Warnings from Tozer to The Church

A. W. Tozer

& Caleb Sinclair

GRAPEVINE INDIA

Published by

GRAPEVINE INDIA PUBLISHERS PVT LTD

www.grapevineindia.com
Delhi | Mumbai
email: grapevineindiapublishers@gmail.com

Ordering Information:
Quantity sales: Special discounts are available on quantity
purchases by corporations, associations, and others.
For details, reach out to the publisher.

First published by Grapevine India 2022

Introduction

Tozer once described himself as a loving father who disciplines his children for their betterment and growth. I do not know if he would appreciate the use of the word 'warnings' in the title. But he would agree that his messages are warnings—or stern words of rebuke, at the least.

We are content to live a lackluster life and never push on to greatness. We do not thirst for God's presence. We try as best we can to make the world and Christ go together. We have set some imaginary standard for ourselves, one that we can effortlessly reach, and we think that it is quite enough. For, we think, we really wish to be classified as crazy fanatics? That is exactly what we will be if we follow the Bible to the letter!

So, we compromise. Since the birth of the Christian faith two thousand years ago, we are always tempted to dilute biblical truth. Tozer sets up a mirror for us to see ourselves in. The sight is not meant to be a pleasant one, but jarring, meant to shake us out of complacency. I pray it will have that effect on yours.

– Caleb Sinclair

1.Keeping The Enemy Out

Human nature tends to excesses by a kind of evil magnetic attraction. We instinctively run to one of two extremes, and that is why we are so often in error.

A proof of this propensity to extremes is seen in the attitude of the average Christian toward the devil. I have observed among spiritual persons a tendency either to ignore him altogether, or to make too much of him. Both are wrong.

There is in the world an enemy whom we dare not ignore. We see him first in the third chapter of Genesis and last in the twentieth of Revelation; which is to say that he was present at the beginning of human history and will be there at its earthly close.

This enemy is not a creation of religious fancy, not a mere personification of evil for convenience, but a being as real as man himself. The Bible attributes to him qualities of personality too detailed to be figurative, and reveals him speaking and acting in situations hard and practical and far removed from the poetic imagination.

The devil is declared in the Scriptures to be an enemy of God and of all good men. He is said to be a liar, a deceiver and a murderer who achieves his ends by guile and trickery. Because he is a spirit, he is able to "walk up and down in the earth" at his pleasure. While he is not omnipresent (omnipresence being an attribute of God alone), he is ubiquitous, which for his purpose amounts to the same thing.

The enemy bears many names, among them being the dragon, the serpent, the devil and Satan.

In addition to this one supreme evil being there are demons, "principalities," "powers," "rulers of the darkness of this world" and "wicked spirits in high places" which operate under his direction. How successful this band of cosmic outlaws has been is written into human history with a pen dipped in blood. The havoc they have wrought in the earth is so frightful as to exceed all power of description. Every newspaper, every news broadcast is a proof of the existence of that evil genius called the devil and his band of vicious spirits dedicated to destruction.

Satan hates God for His own sake, and everything that is dear to God he hates for the very reason that God loves it. Because man was made in God's image, the hatred with which Satan regards him is particularly malevolent. And, since the Christian is doubly dear to God, he is hated by the powers of darkness with an aggravated fury probably not equaled anywhere else in the moral universe.

In view of this, it cannot be less than folly for us Christians to disregard the reality and presence of the enemy. To live in a world under siege is to live in constant peril. To live there and be wholly unaware of the peril is to increase it a hundredfold and to turn the world into a paradise for fools.

While we must not underestimate the strength of the foe, we must at the same time be careful not to fall under his evil spell and live in constant fear of him. "We are not ignorant of his devices." If he cannot make skeptics of us, he will make us devil-conscious and thus throw a permanent shadow across our lives.

There is but a hairline between truth and superstition. We should learn the truth about the enemy, but we must stand bravely against every superstitious notion he would introduce about himself. The truth will set us free, but superstition will enslave us.

I know Christians so engrossed with the fight against evil spirits that they are in a state of constant turmoil. Their touching effort to hold the devil at bay exhausts them nervously and physically, and they manage to stay alive only by frantically calling on God and rebuking the devil in the name of Christ.

These are innocent spiritists in reverse, and are devil-conscious to a point of being borderline neurotics. They grow sensitive and suspicious and always manage to locate an evil spirit as the cause back of everything that irritates them. Then their hackles stand straight up and they begin to order the devil about in a loud voice, but their nervous gestures tell how deeply frightened they are.

The bad thing about all this is that it is contagious. It will soon turn a joyous, worshipful congregation into a crowd of seared and jumpy persons, nervous and completely unhappy.

The scriptural way to see things is to set the Lord always before us, put Christ in the center of our vision. If Satan is lurking around, he will appear only on the margin, and be seen as but a shadow on the edge of the brightness. It is always wrong to reverse this—to set Satan in the focus of our vision and push God out to the margin. Nothing but tragedy can come of such inversion.

The best way to keep the enemy out is to keep Christ in. The sheep need not be terrified by the wolf; they have but to stay dose to the shepherd. It is not the praying sheep Satan fears but the presence of the shepherd.

The instructed Christian whose faculties have been developed by the Word and the Spirit will not fear the devil. When necessary, he will stand against the powers of darkness and overcome them by the blood of the Lamb and the word of his testimony. He will recognize the peril in which he lives and he will know what to do about it, but he will practice the presence of God and never allow himself to become devil-Conscious.

2.No Witness of the Spirit

One cause of the decline in the quality of religious experience among Christians these days is the neglect of the doctrine of the inward witness.

We have emerged shivering from the long period of the theological deep-freeze, stamping our feet to start the circulation and blowing on our hands to limber them up. But the influence of the frosty years is still felt among us, to such an extent that the words *witness, experience* and *feeling* are cautiously avoided by the rank and file of evangelical teachers.

In spite of the undeniable lukewarmness of most of us, we still fear that we shall surely lose our dignity and become howling fanatics by this time next week unless we keep a careful check on ourselves. We set a watch upon our emotions day and night, lest we become over-spiritual and bring reproach upon the cause of Christ.

Which all, if I may say so, is for most of us about as sensible as throwing a cordon of police around a cemetery to prevent a wild political demonstration by the inhabitants.

We who hold the doctrines of the New Testament these days believe ourselves to be in direct lineal descent from the apostles, and true and legitimate offspring of the Early Church. Well, I believe there are today some who do belong to the household of God, who are of the chosen generation and make up the royal priesthood and the holy nation of which Peter writes. They are found scattered among the churches where, we may as well admit, they are often a source of embarrassment to the mixed multitude that composes the membership.

That much is true; but for us to assume that all evangelicals belong in the apostolic succession is to be too optimistic for our own good. To believe so suggests a disquieting parallel with the scribes and Pharisees of Jesus' day. They claimed spiritual descent from Abraham because they could demonstrate that they were his physical offspring. "We be Abraham's seed," they boasted.

Jesus replied by making a distinction. "I know that ye are Abraham's seed," He told them. "If ye were Abraham's children, ye would do the works of Abraham."

In the same way as the Pharisees, we may err gravely by assuming that we are children of God because we hold the creed of God. It most certainly does not follow. It is not physical descent that marks one a true child of Abraham, for Abraham is the father of such as have faith, and faith is not passed on by natural procreation. Similarly it is not creedal descent that proves us to be true sons of Pentecost, but identity of spirit with them upon whose heads sat the cloven tongues like as of fire.

One distinguishing mark of those first Christians was a supernatural radiance that shined out from within them. The sun had come up in their hearts, and its warmth and light made unnecessary any secondary sources of assurance. They had the inner witness. They knew with an immediate awareness that required no jockeying of evidence to give them a feeling of certainty. Great power and great grace marked their lives, enabling them to rejoice to suffer shame for the name of Jesus.

It is obvious that the average evangelical Christian today is without this radiance. The efforts of some of our teachers to cheer up our drooping spirits are futile because those same teachers reject the very phenomenon that would naturally produce joy, namely, the inner witness. In their strange fear of the religious emotions, they have explained away the Scriptures that teach this witness, such as, "The Spirit itself beareth witness" and "He that believeth on the Son of God hath the witness in himself."

Instead of the inner witness, we now substitute logical conclusions drawn from texts. A conversation between a seeker and a worker in an inquiry room is likely to run about like this:

"Do you want the Lord to receive you and make you His child?"

"Yes."

"Well, read this: 'Him that cometh to me I will in no wise cast out.' Do you believe that?"

"Yes?"

"Now if He doesn't cast you out, what does He do?"

"I suppose He takes me in."

"Amen. Now He has taken you in and you are His child. Why don't you tell others about it?"

So the bewildered seeker forces a waxy smile and testifies that he has been converted to Christ. He is honest and means well, but he has been led astray. He has fallen victim to a Spiritless logic. Such assurance as he has rests upon a shaky syllogism. There is no witness, no immediacy of knowledge, no encounter with God, no awareness of inner change.

Where there is a divine act within the soul, there will always be a corresponding awareness. This act of God is self-validating. It is its own evidence and addresses itself direct to the religious consciousness.

Abundant external evidence may exist that a work has been done within, and in this the reason may rejoice. But such evidence cannot be sufficient to guarantee that a saving work has been wrought. Whatever can be judged by reason is subject to the limitations and errors of reason. God waits to assure us that we are His children in a manner that eliminates the possibility of error, that is, by the inner witness.

In one of the most triumphant hymns ever written, "Arise, My Soul, Arise," by Charles Wesley, there occur these lines,

> *"His Spirit answers to the blood,*
>
> *And tells me I am born of God."*

To the salvation-by-logical-conclusion devotees, such language is plain heresy. If it is heresy, I run to join such a glorious heretic. And may God send us many more.

3.An Absent God

"There are over many who have much knowledge and little virtue," said the blind saint, Malaval, "and who often speak of God while rarely speaking to Him."

These words were written a long time ago. Whether they were true of Christians in Malaval's day I am not able to say, as we have but his word for it. But I can testify that they describe vast numbers of Christians today.

The Bible teaches plainly enough the doctrine of the divine omnipresence, but for the masses of professed Christians this is the era of the Absentee God. Most Christians speak of God in the manner usually reserved for a departed loved one, rarely as of one present; but they do not often speak to Him.

Since errors are not equally harmful, I suppose it is better to think of God as existing in some remote region of a lonely universe than not to think of Him at all or, worse, to deny outright that there is any such being as God. But truth is always better than error, and with the inspired Scriptures before us we need not think wrongly about such an important matter as this. We can know the truth if we will.

An Absentee God is among other things inadequate. He does not meet the needs of the being that is called *man*. As a baby is not satisfied away from its mother, and as life on earth is impossible without the sun, so human beings need a present God, and they can be neither healthy nor satisfied without Him. Surely God would not have created us to be satisfied with nothing less than His presence if He had intended that we should get on with nothing more than His absence. No. The Scriptures and moral reason agree that God is present.

Adam and his wife hid themselves from the presence of the Lord among the trees of the garden. Their fear and chagrin for the moment overcame their conscious need of God. Sin never feels comfortable in the divine Presence. Jonah, in his determined refusal to obey God's command, rose up to flee to Tarshish from the presence of the Lord. Peter, with a sudden acute consciousness of personal guilt, sought not to flee from the Lord's presence but begged the Lord instead to depart from him. Men need God above everything else, yet are uncomfortable in His presence. This is the self-contradictory moral situation sin has brought us into.

A convinced atheist is more logical than a Christian who tries to worship an Absentee God. The atheist can ignore all moral and religious precepts without fear because he believes that there is no God to call him to account. His mental state is the same as that of a burglar who has talked himself into the belief that there are no policemen, no courts and no jails. Both may enjoy peace of mind for a while—till the truth catches up with them.

The notion that there is a God but that He is comfortably far away is not embodied in the doctrinal statement of any Christian church. Anyone who dared admit that he held such a creed would be considered a heretic and avoided by respectable religious people. But our actions, and especially our spontaneous utterances, reveal our true beliefs better than any conventional creed can do. If we are to judge by these, I think it can hardly be denied that the average Christian thinks of God as being at a safe distance looking the other way.

One advantage gained from thinking of God as being absent is that we may assume that He is pleased with whatever we may be trying to do, as long as it is not downright wicked. There would seem to be no other way to account for the vast amount of religious nonsense being carried on these days in the name of the Lord. Ambitious persons, burned up with desire to promote the kingdom, hatch up religious schemes so moronic as to be altogether beyond credibility, and which would never be believed by serious-minded persons if they were not put on display in every city, town and hamlet throughout the country.

Since Protestants have no pope to keep them in line, and since God is too far away to be consulted, the only limit to our modern religious folly is the amount the people will stand. Present indications are that they will stand plenty and pay for it, too. That the divine method and manner for evangelizing the world and conducting public services are set forth in the Holy Scriptures never seems to occur to the busy planners whom an Absentee God has left in charge of His affairs while he is away.

At the far end of the spectrum are the conventional churches. I think it is the deep-seated notion that God is absent that makes so many of our church services so insufferably dull. When true believers gather around a present Christ, it is all but impossible to have a poor meeting. The drabbest sermon may be endured cheerfully when the sweet fragrance of Christ's presence fills the room. But nothing can save a meeting held in the name of an Absentee God.

4.Wasted Motion

There is probably not another field of human activity where there is so much waste as in the field of religion.

It is altogether possible to waste an hour in church or even in a prayer meeting. The popular "attend the church of your choice" signs that have lately been appearing everywhere may have some small value if they do no more than remind a materialistic civilization that this world is not all and that there are some treasures that cannot be bought with money. Yet we must not forget that a man may attend church for a lifetime and be none the better for it.

In the average church, we hear the same prayers repeated each Sunday year in and year out with, one would suspect, not the remotest expectation that they will be answered. It is enough, it seems, that they have been uttered. The familiar phrase, the religious tone, the emotionally loaded words have their superficial and temporary effect, but the worshiper is no nearer to God, no better morally and no surer of heaven than he was before.

Yet, every Sunday morning for twenty years, he goes through the same routine allowing two hours for him to leave his house, sit through a church service and return to his house again. He has wasted more than 170 twelve-hour days with this exercise in futility.

The writer to the Hebrews says that some professed Christians were marking time and getting nowhere. They had had plenty of opportunity to grow, but they had not grown; they had had sufficient time to mature, yet they were still babes; so he exhorted them to leave their meaningless religions round and press on to perfection (Heb. 5:11-6:3).

It is possible to have motion without progress, and this describes much of the activity among Christians today. It is simply lost motion.

In God there is motion, but never wasted motion; He always works toward a predetermined end. Being made in His image, we are by nature constituted so that we are justifying our existence only when we are working with a purpose in mind.

Aimless activity is beneath the worth and dignity of a human being. Activity that does not result in progress toward a goal is wasted. Yet, most Christians have no clear end toward which they are striving. On the endless religious merry-go-round, they continue to waste time and energy, of which, God knows, they never had much and have less each hour. This is a tragedy worthy of the mind of an Aeschylus or a Dante.

Back of this tragic waste there is usually one of three causes: The Christian is either ignorant of the Scriptures, unbelieving or disobedient.

I think most Christians are simply uninstructed. They may have been talked into the kingdom when they were only half-ready. Any convert made within the last thirty years was almost certainly told that he had but to take Jesus as his personal Savior and all would be well. Possibly some counselor may have added that he now had eternal life and would most surely go to heaven when he died, if indeed the Lord does not return and carry him away in triumph before the unpleasant moment of death arrives.

After that first hurried entrance into the kingdom, there is usually not much more said. The new convert finds himself with a hammer and a saw, and no blueprint. He has not the remotest notion what he is supposed to build, so he settles down to the dull routine of polishing his tools once each Sunday and putting them back in their box.

Sometimes, however, the Christian wastes his efforts because of unbelief. Possibly we are all guilty of this to some degree. In our private prayers and in our public services we are forever asking God to do things that He either has already done or cannot do because of our unbelief. We plead for Him to speak when He has already spoken and is at that very moment speaking. We ask Him to come when He is already present and waiting for us to recognize Him. We beg the Holy Spirit to fill us while all the time we are preventing Him by our doubts.

Of course, the Christian can hope for no manifestation of God while he lives in a state of disobedience. Let a man refuse to obey God on some dear point, let him set his will stubbornly to resist any commandment of Christ, and the rest of his religious activities will be wasted. He may go to church for fifty years to no profit. He may tithe, teach, preach, sing, write or edit or run a Bible conference till he gets too old to navigate and have nothing but ashes at the last. "To obey is better than sacrifice."

I need only add that all this tragic waste is unnecessary. The believing Christian will relish every moment in church and will profit by it. The instructed, obedient Christian will yield to God as the clay to the potter, and the result will be not waste but glory everlasting.

5.Contemporary Hindrances

Every Christian faces some hindrance in seeking the presence of God. Contemporary Christianity is so taken up by the world that pressing on to the deep things of God becomes rather difficult. Our contemporary times stand in the way of anybody taking his or her spiritual life seriously. So many things are thrown at us; it takes a very resilient soul to resist the onslaught.

Perhaps the most dangerous situation confronting Christians today is what I call *cauterizing the conscience*, that is, making a person insensitive or callous to the world around him. In practical terms, he experiences a deadening of feelings toward morals.

Quite simply, this *moral insensibility* is a lack of feeling. You cannot feel the whole moral question. The strange paradox is that a person may be troubled by his inability to feel, yet he cannot feel. Even among those who consider themselves Christians, there is very little outrage at the immorality of our times.

The source of this dangerous condition is the semi-anesthetization caused by the act of sinning. When a person sins, he anesthetizes his conscience, to a certain extent. If you cauterize a thing, it will hurt at first, but after it heals over, you have no feeling there. Where the cauterization took place, there will develop a hard shell, a thick skin.

Sin does that. It cauterizes the conscience, and soon it does not bother us that we are sinning. This is the work of the blinding agent of the unholy one we call the devil. I do believe in the devil and that he blinds the minds of those who believe not, lest the light of the glorious gospel of Christ might shine onto them (see 2 Cor. 4:4).

Then there is *spiritual lethargy*, an unnatural inward drowsiness when faced with the claims of God. Yet, we hear a speech on the dangers of our times and we immediately want to know how we can get to a fall-out shelter. We hear a program on cancer, and we examine ourselves and wonder if that last pain was a cancer. We are always concerned about superficial things but rarely concerned about spiritual things.

Thomas à Kempis wisely observed, "We give all our attention to things that do us little good, or none at all; things that are vitally necessary we don't bother about them, just give them the go-by. Yes, all that goes to make man drives him to meddle with outward things, and if he doesn't soon recover his senses, is only too glad to wallow in material interests and pleasures."

Moral insensitivity and *spiritual lethargy* are two great curses because they keep us from taking earnest heed to our spiritual health. Unless we are serious about our approach to God, we will be hindered every step of the way. These two things can only be corrected by a sound conversion to Jesus Christ.

Then there is the *preoccupation with making a living*. Jesus called it the "cares of this life" (see Matt. 13:22). If everyone would put as much earnest time and give as much serious attention to seeking God as they put into making a living, they would become a much finer Christian, and soon people would wonder what happened. If women would give as much earnest heed to the claims of Christ and to the needs of their own soul as they give to their house, their cooking and their family, at the end of the week they would have made such spiritual advances that they would be ashamed of the way they had been living before.

The simple fact is that God gets the leftovers, never the main meal. God never gets anything new. He gets the hand-me-downs. We give to God that which we do not need, instead of giving to Him that which we need and thus earning a crown for ourselves. If we were as concerned with our spiritual condition as we are with our homes and our businesses and our income, we would go forward spiritually at a great rate.

The beautiful thing about it is that we would not neglect our homes to do it, and we would not neglect our businesses to do it. You do not have to choose between making a living and going forward with God. You can do both. There is time to do both. You do not have to choose between keeping your house decent and cooking your meals for your husband, and going on with God. You can do both.

An excellent example was a woman by the name of Susannah Wesley, who had nineteen children. John Wesley was the eighteenth child. She kept that house spic-and-span and was known as one of the greatest women of faith of her time. She decided she could look after her family and still make spiritual progress. Her domestic duties did not distract her in the least from her spiritual pursuits.

The same goes for students. If they would seek the face of God as earnestly as they seek books, they would find themselves growing in grace like grass by the watercourses.

Another hindrance is the *constant seeking after pleasure*. There are the physical pleasures: comforts, various vices, food and the rest. And there are mental pleasures, such as social pleasures, gambling and amusements and the reading of fiction. There are aesthetic pleasures: art, music, higher learning and sophisticated culture.

All these put together simply give pleasant sensations, the same sensation a baby gets by sucking his thumb. The whole human race has simply grown-up seeking pleasure, so that we are a race of grownup thumb-suckers. We give over our time to acquiring a pleasant sensation when we ought to give over our time to the advancing of our souls.

Peter says, *"Save yourselves from this untoward generation."* (Acts 2:40)

We may not be in earnest, but God is in dead earnest. God, the Father, was in earnest when He planned and finally accomplished the work of redemption. God, the Son, was in earnest when He sweat great drops of blood in the garden of Gethsemane. And God, the Holy Ghost, is always in earnest when He comes to dwell in the nature of men.

We ought to give the more earnest heed lest we drift away from it; lest we should let it slip. If you will notice in the margin of some Bibles, it says, "Lest that anytime we should let them slip" and "run out as a leaking vessel." Other versions have "we should drift away from it." A great many people have leaking hearts and spirits.

We neglect "so great salvation" by drifting from it. And how do we neglect it? We get the truth in our heart, but we let it leak away. It is a heartbreaking truth that some hearts are leaky, and their good resolutions all trickle away.

People remain sober until New Year's and then on New Year's Eve, they lose their sobriety and start making resolutions. "I resolve that I will be kinder to my wife this year." "I resolve that I will give regularly to the church." "I resolve that I will pray regularly every day." "I resolve that I will not let a day go by that I do not read the Holy Scriptures." "I resolve that I will seek to know God better." "I resolve . . ."

But the heart is a leaky thing, and before the first of February, the average person's resolutions have all evaporated. The good intentions, the strong wine of spiritual desire when you heard a man preach whose words touched you particularly; suddenly you can see the strong desire for God. And you long after the strong wine of spiritual desire, but your heart is like a sieve, and pretty soon it all leaks away. Soon there is no desire left at all.

The difference between spiritual things and earthly things is that the things of the spirit are so modest. The things of the spirit are not pushing in on you; they are not singing commercials to you; they are not knocking on your door and urging you to buy; they are simply waiting for you to notice.

Jesus did not lift up His voice nor make Himself heard in the street. He did not cry aloud, but was calm and quiet. People came to Him for the truth.

But the things of the flesh are so insistent, so clamorous. Before you are up in the morning, they are clamoring at you, trying to get you interested in buying what they are selling or doing what they have decided you should do. Everybody is singing to you, urging you, pushing you—by example, by precept, by instruction, by advertising and urging—trying to get you to go certain ways and do certain things.

Our Lord is never intrusive; but the things of the world are intrusive. Here is the point I am trying to make: If you are going to give attention to the things of God and save your own soul, you are going to have to have a good intention, a good resolution and then see to it that you do it. Do not let the devil prevent you. You are going to have to take yourself by the scruff of the neck, shake yourself and say, "Now, I don't know what others are going to do, but as for me, I'm going to seek the face of God. I'm going to see if I can be a better man next week than I was last week, and a better man next month than I was last month."

God meant it when He gave us the Law. Christ meant it when He died and rose on the third day. The Holy Ghost means it when He quietly speaks to your heart. How much more will we be judged if we heed not the truth that they were judged that heeded not the Law?

"For if the word spoken by angels was steadfast, and every transgression and disobedience received a just recompense of reward; how shall we escape, if we neglect so great salvation; which at the first began to be spoken by the Lord, and was confirmed unto us by them

that heard him; God also bearing them witness, both with signs and wonders, and with divers miracles, and gifts of the Holy Ghost, according to his own will?" (Heb. 2:2-4)

Some confess, "I intended to . . . later." However, there was no later time.

"I didn't understand," they say. But they understood enough at the time.

"I was too busy." But at last they found time to die.

Somebody else says, "Nobody in my crowd paid any attention to these things," but it is always so. The saving voice of God speaks to a crowd of men, but only one here and there hears it. When the voice of God spoke to the antediluvian world, only Noah and his family heard it. The rest of them perished in the flood.

Somebody else says, "If I pay attention to this, I'll lose my job." Chances are, you will not, but if you do, any job you lose saving your soul certainly will be a wonderful bargain. Somebody else says, "I want to have some fun yet. And then I'll become a Christian." I will not answer that. It is too meaningless, too lacking in significance to warrant any serious answer. Another says, "I was afraid of what people would say." Afraid of what *people* would say? What about what God says?

Society is in an elaborate conspiracy to make us alike. Society is in a conspiracy to make us all bad; not too bad, because if we get too bad, we become a problem to the police. But not too good, for if we get too good, we are fanatical, so they say. So society wants to keep us nice, trimmed down, going to church, supporting boys' clubs and girls' clubs and hospitals.

Certainly, those things are all right. The general society wants to keep us just good enough not to be a problem to the police, but bad enough not to bother their conscience.

I hear the voice of God calling us to a higher kind of life. The book of Hebrews is an urgent, vibrant, living book that speaks to those that are on the border and says, "Go on over. You can dare to do it. Go on over." And it speaks to those who could not quite make up their minds whether they wanted to obey and believe God, and says, "You dare obey. You dare believe."

Whatever causes us to overcome all hindrances is handsomely rewarded when we break through to the glorious sunshine of His blessed presence.

Love Divine, All Love Excelling

by Charles Wesley (1707–1788)

Love divine, all love excelling,

Joy of heaven, to earth come down;

Fix in us thy humble dwelling;

All thy faithful mercies crown.

Jesus, thou art all compassion,

Pure, unbounded love thou art;

Visit us with thy salvation,

Enter every trembling heart.

Breathe, oh, breathe thy Holy Spirit

Into every troubled breast;

Let us all thy grace inherit;

Let us find thy promised rest;

Take away the love of sinning;

Take our load of guilt away;

End the work of thy beginning;

Bring us to eternal day.

Carry on thy new creation;

Pure and holy may we be;

Let us see our whole salvation

Perfectly secured by thee;

Change from glory into glory,

Till in heaven we take our place,

Till we cast our crowns before thee,

Lost in wonder, love, and praise.

6.Refining Sin Without Removing

We Christians must look sharp that our Christianity does not simply refine our sins without removing them.

The work of Christ as Savior is twofold: to "save his people from their sins", and to reunite them forever with the God from whom sin had alienated them.

God's holy character requires that He refuse to admit sin into His fellowship. Mercy may pardon the returning sinner and place him judicially beyond the reach of the broken law through the redemption which is in Christ Jesus. But neither the boundless grace nor the infinite kindness of God can make it morally congruous for a pure being to have communion with an impure one. It is necessary to the moral health of the universe that God divide the light from the darkness and that He say at last to every sinner, "Depart from me, ye that work iniquity."

This certainly is no new thought. Christian theologians have all recognized the necessity for an adequate purgation of the inner springs of moral conduct and the impartation of a renewed nature to the believer before he is ready for the fellowship of God. Our hymnists also have seen and wrestled with this great problem—and thanks be to God, they have found the answer, too.

Binney felt the weight of this problem and stated it along with the solution in a little known but deeply spiritual hymn:

Eternal Light! eternal Light!

How pure that soul must be

When placed within Thy searching sight,

it shrinks not, but with calm delight

Can live, and look on Thee.

O how shall I, whose native sphere

Is dark, whose mind is dim,

Before the ineffable appear,

And on my naked spirit bear

That uncreated beam?

There is a way for man to rise

To that sublime abode:

An offering and a sacrifice,

A Holy Spirit's energies,

An Advocate with God.

The offering and the sacrifice and the sanctifying energies of the Holy Spirit are indeed sufficient to prepare the soul for communion with God. The Bible declares this, and ten thousand times ten thousand witnesses confirm it. The big danger is that we assume that we have been delivered from our sins, when in reality we have only exchanged one kind of sin for another. This is the peril that lies in wait for everyone. It need not discourage us nor turn us back, but it should make us watchful.

We must, for instance, be careful that our repentance is not simply a change of location. Whereas we once sinned in the far country among the swineherds, we are now chumming with religious persons, considerably cleaner and much more respectable in appearance, to be sure, but no nearer to true heart purity than we were before.

Again, by religious influence, pride may be refined to quiet self-esteem. It may be skillfully dissembled by a neat use of Bible words that meant everything to those who first used them, but which only serves to disguise deep self-love which is to God a hateful and intolerable thing. The real trouble is thus not cleared up, but only driven underground.

The gossip and troublemaker sometimes at conversion turns into a "spiritual counselor," but often a closer look will reveal the same restless, inquisitive spirit at work that made her a nuisance before her conversion. The whole thing has been refined and given a religious appearance, but actually nothing radical has happened. She is still running the same stand, only on the other side of the street.

There has been a certain refinement of the sin, but definitely not a removal of it. This is Satan's most successful way of getting into the church to cause weakness, backsliding and division.

Many business transactions which among worldly men we would brand as sharp practice, are hailed as a remarkable answer to prayer and a proof that God is a "partner" in the affair, when they are carried out by a Christian after he has prayed over it.

These are illustrations only, intended to show how sin may alter its appearance without changing its nature, and are not to be taken to mean that I am opposed to Christian counselors or businessmen who pray over their affairs. The contrary is true. That church is blessed indeed which has in it a few persons with the gift of discernment to whom weak and troubled Christians may come for help in times of crisis. And blessed is the businessman today who has learned to pray his way through red tape and taxes. Without the help of God, I do not see how businessmen stay sane in this frightful rat race we call civilization.

The temptation to spare the best of the sheep and the cattle is very strong in all of us. Like Saul before us we are willing enough to slay the scrubby sheep and the old sway-back steers, but Adam and the devil join to try to persuade us to keep the fattest beasts alive. And many of us fall for the old trick. We make pets of the cattle we should have destroyed and their bleatings and bellowings are heard throughout all Christendom.

The will of God is that sin should be removed, not merely refined. Let's walk in His will.

7.Self-Trust

Trust in the LORD with all thine heart;

and lean not unto thine own understanding.

In all thy ways acknowledge him,

and he shall direct thy paths.

PROVERBS 3:5-6

Paul was a man who knew what he believed and where he stood. He knew God and was confident with a great cosmic confidence, yet that same man was the most distrustful of himself. As great as Paul was, he did not trust himself.

Before man, Paul was as bold as a lion. But before God, Paul could not say too much against himself. When he was in front of God, Paul actually had no confidence in himself at all. His confidence with God was in reverse proportion to his confidence in himself. The amount of self-trust Paul had was as little as the trust he had in God was great.

What do I mean by "self-trust"? Simply, it is the respectability and self-assurance that comes through education. It is what you learn about yourself and what your friends tell you about yourself and all the best that you may give yourself. Self-trust is the last great obstacle to living the crucified life, which is why we mill around the deep river of God like animals around a waterhole, afraid to go in because the water may be too deep. We never quite get it.

I want to quote a little from a man who had a wonderful name: Lorenzo Scupoli (1530–1610). He was one of those strange Catholics who, during his lifetime, was considered more or less a heretic because of his evangelical leaning.

He wrote a book called *The Spiritual Combat*, which is a practical manual for living. Scupoli begins by teaching that the essence of life is continually fighting against our egoistic longings. Scupoli says the way to win the fight is to replace our desires for self-gratification with acts of charity and sacrifice. The one who does not do this loses and suffers eternity in hell. The one who does it, trusting not in his own strength but in God's power, triumphs and will be happy in heaven.

Scupoli analyzes several common, real-life situations and advises on how to cope with each of them to keep your conscience clear and to improve your virtue. Anyone who continues to act against God is the cause of all that is bad. All good comes from God, whose goodness is limitless. Scupoli wrote:

So necessary is self-distrust in this conflict, that without it you will be unable, I say not to achieve the victory desired, but even to overcome the very least of your passions. Let this be well impressed upon your mind; for our corrupt nature too easily inclines us to a false estimate of ourselves; so that, being really nothing, we account ourselves to be something, and presume, without the slightest foundation, upon our own strength.

This is a fault not easily discerned by us, but very displeasing in the sight of God. For He desires and loves to see in us a frank and true recognition of this most certain truth, that all the virtue and grace which is within us is derived from Him alone, Who is the fountain of all good, and that nothing good can proceed from us, no, not even a thought which can find acceptance in His sight.

Why is self-trust so wrong? Self-trust is wrong because it robs God. God says, *"Will a man rob God? Yet ye have robbed me. But ye say, Wherein have we robbed thee? In tithes and offerings."* (Mal. 3:8)

We have robbed God and taken away from Him what belongs to Him. Paul states that God is the fountain of all, and nothing, not even good thoughts, can come from us unless they come from God first (see Rom. 11:35-36). If you ignore the fact that God is the source of everything and make a converted and sanctified self the source, it is just as bad as it can be because final trust in God has been taken away. The self judges God and man and holds God to be less than He is and man to be more than he is. This is our trouble.

Study theology and learn about how God is the source and fountain of all things. Learn about the attributes of God and see if, in your heart, you still believe that God is less than He is and you are more than you are.

Think of the moon. If the moon could talk like a man and have a personality, it could say within itself, *I shine on the earth and every time I'm around, the earth becomes beautiful.* If someone could respond to the moon, they would say, "Listen, you don't do that by yourself. Don't you know that you have been discovered and found out? You don't shine at all. You are simply reflecting the sun's light, so it's really the sun that shines."

Then self comes to the rescue of the moon. "You're letting your light shine and you're doing a good job," it says. "When you're not up, one whole side of the earth lies in darkness. But when you come up, a side lights up and I can begin to see rows of houses. You're doing a fine job."

The moon would not say, "The glory belongs to God, because it is only by the grace of God that I'm like this." All the time the moon is thinking that he is shining.

When the moon is shining, it is only a reflection light from the sun. And if the moon really understood, he could boldly shine and talk about it, because he would know that he was not shining at all. Similarly, Paul knew that he did not have a thing of himself that was fit for heaven. He had only the grace of God in him. It was God and not him. He completely and radically distrusted himself. No man can really know himself; he is not capable of knowing how he feels.

Everybody thinks they know what they sound like until they hear themselves on a recording. One of the most humbling things that ever happened to me was when I had a sermon recorded. For the first time I heard the sound of my own voice, and that recording did not lie to me. Up to that time, I had been told I had a fine preaching voice. Then I heard myself, and nobody needs to talk to me about *that* anymore.

I have listened to myself, and I know how I sound. No man knows the sound of his own voice until he hears it, and no man knows how weak he is until God exposes him and nobody wants to be exposed.

It is important that we understand how dangerous it is to trust our good habits and virtues. Only God can bring us to the point of understanding that our strength is indeed our weakness. Anything that we rely on or trust can be our undoing. We do not realize how weak we are until the Holy Spirit begins exposing these things to us.

The question I must pose is simply, how do we learn this self-distrust? Basically, God uses four different ways to deal with this matter. These are supported and confirmed by the devotional writers, the great hymnists and the Christian biographers. They weave like a common thread through the lives of those who are committed to living the crucified life.

I believe the first and best way to deal with self-trust is for God to *flash some holy inspiration into your soul and expose it.*

This has happened to many people. For example, it happened to Brother Lawrence. In *The Practice of the Presence of God*, he wrote that for 40 years he was never once out of the conscious presence of God: "When I took the cross and decided to obey Jesus and walk this holy way, I gathered that I would have to suffer a lot."

Then he said something rather strange: "For some reason God never found me worthy of much suffering. He just let me continue to trust Him and I put all my self trust away and I have been trusting in God completely." Brother Lawrence was living the crucified life, believing Christ was in him, around him and near him. And he was praying all the time.

God flashed some holy inspiration into the heart of Lady Julian of Norwich, and because of the revelations she received, she knew instantly that she was no good and that Jesus Christ was everything. She stayed in that position until she died.

I think this is probably the easiest way for us to get it—for the Lord to give us a sweet, sudden burst of holy inspiration within our hearts that shows us the real self. Of course, this is where our doctrine gets in our way. We can believe the whole counsel of God, and our life may still be plagued with pride to such an extent that it hides the face of God. It is such pride that prevents us from going forward in victory.

This cannot be corrected by a lecture on correct doctrine. Rather, we need the Holy Spirit to tell us the true condition of our soul. We need Him to reveal to us how bad we really are and lead us out of our spiritual swamp.

Another way in which God deals with our self-trust is *the physical realm*. Many people have a hard time believing that God would actually bring physical harm to our bodies. Yet the Scriptures bear out the fact that physical pain is one of God's effective means of dealing with an undisciplined self.

The Old Testament is filled with examples of physical suffering imposed by God, but probably Job stands out above all the rest. A casual reading of Job's story may not get to the real problem that Job had. Certainly, he was a good man, and the Scriptures bear this out. The problem with Job was that he was a good man and he knew it. If you are good but you do not know it, then God can use you. However, if you know how good and great you are, you cease to be a vehicle through which God can send His blessing.

The only way God could get to the center of Job's problem was through physical pain. Sometimes this is the only way He can get our attention. God is not above using this method to deal with the problems of pride and self-trust. And the suffering God sends will sometimes not be curable by any medicine. Of course, the only cure for such a physical ailment is renouncing the self and humbling ourselves before God.

Nobody likes to talk about this sort of thing today. Everybody wants to hear happy, cheerful inspirational thoughts that make us feel good. This is why to get a crowd to come to church today, we need a cowbell, a musical saw or a talking horse to have some fun and a little bit of entertainment for those who are bored with the simple, plain word of God. Nobody wants to hear about physical discipline or pain. After all, we believe in healing.

Another method God uses to develop distrust of ourselves is *extreme trials and temptations*. From listening to some preachers and reading some books, it is easy to conclude that once a person is born again, that is the end of it—no more trials or temptations. Those who believe in the infilling of the Holy Spirit have somehow also communicated the idea that this is the end of all Christian experience. But the Bible tells us that after Jesus was filled with the Spirit, He was driven into the wilderness for some severe temptations.

When a Christian faces a difficult or extreme trial or temptation, he is tempted to throw in the towel and say, "God, it's no use. I'm just no good. You obviously don't want me, so I'm finished." All the while he forgets that God wants to teach us through these trials and temptations that self-trust is dangerous and unreliable.

At times, when something blows up in our face, we think it is all over instead of taking it as proof that we are not mature Christians. We need to take the blowup as proof that we are nearer to our forever home today than we were yesterday. We need to understand that our heavenly Father is letting these things happen to us to wean us away from trusting ourselves and to move us to lean exclusively on the

Lord Jesus Christ.

Some have the idea that repentance is to be a drawn-out affair that includes beating yourself down. I think we need to start with repentance, but there comes a time when we need to just turn everything over to God and then not do it anymore. That is the best repentance in the world. If you did something last week you are ashamed of, feel conviction and condemnation about it, simply say, "I repent." Turn it over to the Lord, tell Him about it, and then do not do it anymore.

What is the purpose of these severe trials and temptations that sometimes cause you to fail? It is not to show you that you are not a true Christian. Rather, it is to show you that your conscience is tender and you are very near to God. The Lord is trying to teach you that last lesson so that you rid yourself of self-distrust. The closer you are to God, the more tender your conscience is before the Lord, and the more severe your trial and temptation may be.

Some in the Church have lied to us by inferring that the Christian life is void of difficulty, problems and trials. The exact opposite is the truth.

The great characters of the Bible shed some light on the subject. Remember Jacob's temptation? Remember Peter's temptation? All throughout Scripture (and all of Church history), there are countless individuals who encountered great trials and temptations. Hebrews 11 tells about many of those heroes of faith—those who endured extreme trials and temptations in life.

Sometimes a trial comes along, and we run to the Bible, pull out a quote and say, "According to this Scripture right here, we got it." We have certain confidence in ourselves. We think we know exactly what is going on. The problem is that we do *not* know what is happening, and so God will deal with our self-trust.

God certainly knows our feelings. He knows we are so proud of the way we rightly divide the word of truth and that we can disjoint a text like a butcher getting a chicken ready for the barbecue. With words all carefully laid out and knowing just where to put your finger on this or just where to put your finger on that, you are too smart for God to bless you. You know too much. You can identify everything, but the dear heavenly Father knows you do not really know much at all. He lets things happen to you until you recognize that you do not know what is happening. Your friends do not know what is going on either.

And when you go to somebody you feel you can trust, that person will not be able to help you either. That is actually good news.

It truly would be terrible if we had some holy Saint Francis to whom we all could go to find out where we were, what was happening to us and what life is all about. God loves us too much for that. He is trying to teach us to trust Him, not people—to lean on Him, not on people. I have been so scared that people would start trusting in me and leaning on me. However, fear not! God pulls the crutches out from under me occasionally, just to see if He can trust me.

As a Christian, you know some of the means God uses to teach His people. As a Christian, you love God, but you are sick of all the nonsense in the world. You are sick of all the nonsense in the Church. Your heart is crying after God just as the doe yearns after the water brooks. Your heart and your flesh cry out for the living God. Yet in spite of all this, you still trust yourself. You testify that you love your Bible and that your time of prayer is precious, but still your tendency is to trust yourself.

This tendency is more difficult to deal with because we do not talk about this anymore. This teaching left the evangelical and fundamental church a generation ago. Nowadays when someone becomes a Christian, everybody slaps him on the back and says, "Glory to God, Brother, you are born again!"

Ah, but the Lord says, "That's only the beginning." The Scriptures teach that God will rejoice over us with joy and with singing. This is not a picture of an angry God. Rather, it is a picture of a loving Father who is everlastingly patient toward us, His children. God is not judging us. God only wants His children to grow and develop into full-fledged Christians. Sometimes, in order to accomplish this, God must send us through severe and harsh trials and temptations. But the destination is Christian perfection in the person of the Lord Jesus Christ.

I would condense the fourth thing God uses in dealing with our self-trust into one simple thought: *Look around for the saintly footprints where you are right now.* You are not alone in this journey. Look around for footprints and find out who made those footprints. You will notice that the footprints are those of the great saints who lived in ages past.

I am not interested in any of the modern footprints. I am interested only in those footprints that have come to us down through the centuries. If you look around and see these footprints, you will find them all going in the same direction. You will find they follow the footprints of Jesus. They are all going in the same direction. Look carefully and you will see some of them backtracking a little occasionally, but you will also see that they found their way at last and went back to following after Jesus. They are all following Christ.

Now, the absolutely cheerful and confident Christian can expect this very same thing. You want the Lord to do something for you, don't you? You want Him to come down on you with a wave of grace. As a congregation, we want to again see the Reformation or a revival coming down on us with power. We want to see power in our individual lives. We want the Holy Spirit to come on us and demonstrate His power. We want to see all of that, but we need to be careful that we're not trying to work it up on our own.

I do not intend to try to work up anything. You cannot climb Jacob's ladder without sweat, perspiration and hard work. The work of God is not dependent on any man's schedule.

I rarely know where I am going in my life's journey, but after I have been there a year, I can look back and see that my path has been relatively straight. I go to God, write out my prayers, wait on Him and remind Him, but nothing seems to happen. I seem to be getting nowhere, and then suddenly things break around me. I look back and see that God has been leading my every step, and I did not even know it.

I did not know where I was going, but looking back, I can see where I have been. I do not think we should always look back, but at least we should be able to look back and see the terrain where God has led us—the valleys and plateaus He has brought us through because He loves us in spite of ourselves.

The more my trust rests in God, the less I trust myself. If we truly desire to live the crucified life, we must get rid of self-trust and trust only in God.

William W. How (1823–1897)

We give thee but Thine own,

Whate'er the gift may be;

All that we have is Thine alone,

A trust, O Lord, from Thee.

May we Thy bounties thus

As stewards true receive,

And gladly, as Thou blessest us,

To Thee our firstfruits give.

O hearts are bruised and dead,

And homes are bare and cold,

And lambs for whom the Shepherd bled

Are straying from the fold.

To comfort and to bless,

To find a balm for woe,

To tend the lone and fatherless

Is angels' work below.

The captive to release,

To God the lost to bring,

To teach the way of life and peace

It is a Christ-like thing.

And we believe Thy Word,

Though dim our faith may be;

Whate'er for Thine we do, O Lord,

We do it unto Thee.

8.Self-Will

"If it were true the Lord puts the Christian believer on the shelf every time he fails or does something wrong, I would have been a piece of statuary by this time!"

Man's very human habit of trusting in himself is generally the last great obstacle blocking his pathway to victory in Christian experience.

Even the Apostle Paul, writing in his New Testament letters, confessed that his confidence in God was in completely opposite ratio to his confidence in himself. Paul made it very plain that it was only after giving up the last inclination to trust in himself that he became immersed in the sufficiency of Christ.

We can learn much from the experiences of Paul and the humility of his testimony, *"For I know that in me ... dwelleth no good thing."* (Romans 7:18) He had discovered that to be fully surrendered to God and the will of God meant that first he must come to an entire and radical distrust of himself.

After he became willing to look within his own being, Paul had no further confidence in himself and couldn't say enough against himself. But when he went forth before men in the compulsion of ministry for Christ, he seemed to stand sure with a great cosmic confidence because he had met God and could honestly declare that *"we have this treasure in earthen vessels, that the excellency of the power may be of God, and not of us."* (2 Corinthians 4:7)

Paul was being continually thrown into spiritual combat as he moved forward in his declaration of Jesus as Christ and Lord. He knew the blessing and the power of operating from a position of strength—the fact that he held no illusions about himself and depended completely upon the Spirit of God.

"By the grace of God I am what I am," (1 Corinthians 15:10) he said.

"I am the least of the apostles, that am not meet to be called an apostle," (1 Corinthians 15:9) he wrote.

"Christ Jesus came into the world to save sinners; of whom I am chief," (1 Timothy 1:15) he acknowledged.

This all adds up to a startling statement of truth held not only by Paul but by all of the great saints who have done exploits for God. They would all remind us that those who insist on trusting human self will never obtain the desired victory in spiritual combat, for they will presume vainly in their own strength!

To become effective men of God, then, we must know and acknowledge that every grace and every virtue proceeds from God alone, and that not even a good thought can come from us except it be of Him.

I think that most of us can glibly quote the Scriptures about the lessons that Paul learned without actually coming to this place of complete distrust of ourselves and our own strengths. Our self-trust is such a subtle thing that it still comes around whispering to us even after we are sure it is gone.

In our search for God and for victory, perhaps we have put away all the sins that have plagued us. We have tried to deal with all of the self-sins that we know, allowing them to be crucified. At this point we have stopped boasting, and we are sure that we have stopped loving ourselves. It may be that in the process we have humbled ourselves and publicly gone forward to an altar to confess our need and to pray.

Now, this is my caution—after we have humbled ourselves, there is a possibility that our subtle self-trust may prove to be stronger than ever, for it has a better foundation upon which to build! After we have put away our sins and given up our will and after we have taken a position of confession and humility, our self-trust is quick to whisper its consolation deep within us.

Often when this has happened, Christians have made the mistake of believing that this whisper of consolation comes from the Holy Ghost—and that is why we are so weak when we think we are strong!

Just what is the whisper that is likely to come to us deep within our being?

"You have really come a long way, and you have advanced far ahead of others," self-trust is likely to whisper. "You have put sin behind you, and you have humbled yourself. You will be a power for you are not one of the dead ones. You may trust yourself now because you have left much behind, and parted with friends, and paid a price!

You are really getting somewhere. You will have victory now—with God's help, of course!"

I call this a kind of back-scratching—and our old self knows just when to come through with it because it feels so good to us in terms of consolation and comfort. It is the process of reverting right back to self-trust, and almost all of the joy that the average Christian knows is the back-scratching that self gives him.

When self whispers an assurance to you that you are different—look out! "You are different," self whispers, and then adds the proof. "You have given up enough things to make you a separated Christian. You love the old hymns, and you can't stand the modern nonsense. You have a good standard—none of those movies and none of this modern stuff for you!"

You don't really know what is happening to you, but you are feeling pretty good about everything by this time. But the good feeling is strictly from being coddled and comforted and scratched by a self that has refused to die. Self-trust is still there—and you thought it had gone!

Now, what is our great encouragement in view of all that we know about ourselves? It is the fact that God loves us without measure, and He is so keenly interested in our spiritual growth and progress that He stands by in faithfulness to teach and instruct and discipline us as His dear children!

I once wrote something about how God loves us and how dear we are to Him. I wasn't sure I should put it down on paper, but God knew what I meant. I said, "The only eccentricity that I can discover in the heart of God is that a God such as He is should love sinners such as we are!" God has that strange eccentricity, but it still does not answer our wondering question, "Why did God love us?"

On this earth a mother will love the boy who has betrayed her and sinned and is now on his way to life in prison. That seems to be a natural thing for a mother, but there is nothing natural about this love of God. It is a divine thing—it is forced out by the inward pressure within the heart of God. That is why He waits for us, puts up with us, desires to lead us on—He loves us!

You can put all of your confidence in God. He is not angry with you, His dear child! He is not waiting to pounce on you in judgment—He knows that we are dust, and He is loving and patient toward us.

If it were true that the Lord would put the Christian on the shelf every time he failed and blundered and did something wrong, I would have been a piece of statuary by this time! I know God, and He isn't that kind of God. He will bring judgment when judgment is necessary, but the Scriptures say that judgment is God's strange work. Where there is a lifetime of rebellion, hardened unbelief, love of sin and flagrant refusal of His love and grace, judgment will fall. But with His dear children, God watches over us for spiritual growth and maturity, trying to teach us how necessary it is for us to trust in Him completely and to come to a complete distrust of ourselves.

There are at least three ways that God may use to teach us this necessity of completely distrusting ourselves.

Occasionally this lesson from God has come by *holy inspiration*. I suppose the best and easiest way to find out that you are no good is to have God flash that knowledge suddenly into your soul. I know that it has happened to some people. I think of the writings of the saintly Brother Lawrence who testified that God gave him this vision and knowledge of himself in such a way that for years he was never out of the conscious presence of God!

"When I took the cross and decided to obey Jesus and walk in His holy way, I knew that I might be called upon to suffer," Brother Lawrence wrote. "But, for some reason, God never counted me worthy of much suffering. He just let me continue to trust in Him completely after I put all my self-trust away. It is a life of carrying His cross and believing that He is in me and around me and near me, and praying without ceasing."

Lady Julian, also, wrote in her book of the gracious experience when God, by holy inspiration, gave light to her heart so that she realized instantly that she was worthless in herself and that Jesus Christ was everything!

At this point someone is sure to say, "But Mr. Tozer, I already know that I am bad. I am a believer in total depravity!"

My reply is this: It is possible to be a confirmed believer in total depravity and still be as proud as Lucifer! It is possible to believe in depravity and still trust in yourself in such a way that the face of God is hidden and you are kept from victory.

We are dealing with something else here—not theological total depravity. We may not understand how we can inherit evil from our fathers, but there is no argument with the fact that as soon as we are big enough to sin, we go directly into the business of sinning. It has been true of every child of every race and of every nationality—we are born bad, and in that sense, we are all alike.

The lesson that we are trying to draw here is the necessity of God revealing by the Holy Spirit the utter weakness of the child of God who is still putting trust in himself. A teacher can tell you that you are weak and that all of your righteousnesses are but filthy rags and you may still go through school and get a long degree and go out proudly to be a missionary or a preacher or a Bible teacher. Our selfish condition—if we are still trusting in ourselves—can only be demonstrated to us by the Holy Spirit. When the knowledge comes and we lean only on Him, we will know that "conscious presence" in which Brother Lawrence lived and rejoiced continually day by day!

Another way in which we may have to learn this lesson from God is with *harsh scourgings*. Perhaps this makes me appear to belong to the seventeenth century for it does not have a popular sound in our day. We are more likely to bring in the cow bells and try to give everyone a little bit of pleasure than to faithfully declare that our dear heavenly Father may use harsh scourging to teach His children distrust of self.

Actually, I would prefer to preach from the 23rd Psalm every Sunday for a year. Then I would take up the 53rd chapter of Isaiah and after a long time I would come to the 13th chapter of First Corinthians.

But if I should do that, what would happen to my congregation in the meantime? The flock of God would become the softest, sweetest and spongiest group of no-goods that ever came together!

The Lord does have to give us chastening and discipline and harsh scourging at times. None of you would feed your children continually on a diet of sugar cookies—they would lose their teeth! There must be a diet with solid stuff if they are to be vigorous and well.

We speak of harsh scourgings and immediately we think of that man Job in the Old Testament. We have a great deal of pity for Job and in human sympathy many people take Job's part against God—and certainly against his wife! But have you ever noticed that Job was far from being humble, even though he was a praying man and one who made sacrifices because his children might have sinned at their party the night before. But we finally hear him saying in that long discourse, *"Oh, that I were as in months past, as in the days when God preserved me ... when I went out to the gate through the city, when I prepared my seat in the street!"* (Job 29:2, 7)

He was a "big shot," you know, and that is what they did then. They had a place at the head of the street where the honored men were seated.

"The young men saw me, " he said, *"and hid themselves: and the aged arose, and stood up."* (29:8)

Who is this coming down the street? The honorable Mister Job!

"Oh, here I am now, lying in this ash pile," he said. "They have cast me out. No one would vote for me now, but there was a day when princes refrained from talking in my presence and laid their hands on their mouths" (see Job 29:9).

Brother Job was no ordinary rag picker—he was a great man! But he knew it—and that was the trouble and that's why those harsh things happened to him. If you are great and you happen to suspect it, and you are God's child—things will start happening to you, too.

Finally, seeing God's majesty and power, Job said, "Oh God, I have been talking and talking and talking, but now I put my hand over my mouth—I am vile!" (see Job 42:6). It was only then that the Lord could say to him, "All right, Job, now pray for the rest of them!" (see 42:8). So Job prayed for those who had tried to comfort him, and God gave back to him twice as much as he had possessed previously (see 42:10).

There is a third way, also, in which God may be trying to deal with our weakness of self-trust. We are familiar with this method if we study the Bible, for it is the discipline of manifold temptations.

Some Christians are prone to sink into discouragement when called upon to face temptations, but I think that these disciplines should become a spiritual encouragement to us. God does not allow the temptations and testings to come to us because He is trying to show us up—He is dealing with us through this means because we are Christians, we are His children! He is dealing with us in the midst of temptations because He has found our conscience is tender enough to listen and because we are willing to be drawn closer to Him. He is only trying to teach us this necessary lesson of distrust of self.

When temptations come, you are not to throw in the towel and say, "Oh God, I guess this proves that you don't want me!" Instead, it should be a sign to you as you come through the testing by His grace that you are nearer your eternal home today than you were yesterday!

There are scriptural examples of men of God who were sifted in the course of such testing experiences. Think of blustery Peter and his denial of the Savior when wicked men arrested Jesus and put Him through the mockery of a trial before taking Him out to Calvary to be crucified. What if Peter had taken his own actions as proof that he was not really a Christian disciple? It was a difficult course, but it was a most powerful lesson from the heavenly Father, revealing to Peter what an ineffective believer he would be if he continued to trust in his own strength.

None of us can really tell how weak and useless we are until God has exposed us—and no one wants to be exposed! But God knows so much better than we do that He must expose us for our own good.

Neither do any of us really know how unstable we are until we have been exposed by the Holy Ghost. Peter was a big, bold, strong fisherman, and it seemed easy for him to say to the Lord, "Let everyone else run away, but I will always stand by. You can count on me, Master!" I am sure it was hard for him to take the answer that Jesus gave him: "Before the rooster crows tonight you will say three times that you do not know me!" But Jesus knew the instability of the man who still tried to stand in his own strength and in his own self-trust.

We do not really know how unstable we are, and we often refuse to admit the truth when we find out, when we are exposed. That is why it is too dangerous to trust our good habits and our virtues—and that is why our distrust of ourselves must be the work of God's hand!

Oh, brethren, He is our God, and this is my advice—love Him and trust Him and depend only upon Him! If we insist upon trusting ourselves, our training, our education, our talents and our human judgment—we make God less than He is and we make man more than he is! We take the glory from God and give it to our converted and sanctified self—and that is shameful, because it takes from God the ultimate and final trust. Even when we say that we know that God is the Source and the Fountain of all things, and we recite His attributes and become experts in theology, we may still believe in our hearts that we are more than we really are!

This is where we need repentance and forgiveness. I recall that Brother Lawrence, writing about the pattern of victory in the daily walk with God, gave a simple and direct solution to failures and wrongdoing. He advised that if we ever make a slip and do that which is wrong, we should not ignore it and let it remain unconfessed and unforgiven.

"I would go straight to the Lord and say, 'Now Lord, that's me—and if you don't forgive me and help me, that's what you can expect—for that's me!'" is what he wrote in essence. "God forgave me, and I went right on from there."

Some people insist that repentance and forgiveness must be a long, drawn-out affair, but I don't agree that it must necessarily be so. I believe the best repentance is turning to God and away from our sin—and not doing it any longer!

That is the best repentance in the whole wide world. Why does it take us so long to put our complete trust in God when He has made it so simple and so rewarding to yield what we are to Him!

9.Self-Deception

Of all forms of deception, self-deception is the deadliest, and of all deceived persons the self-deceived are the least likely to discover the fraud.

The reason for this is simple. When a man is deceived by another he is deceived against his will. He is contending against an adversary and is temporarily the victim of the other's guile. Since he expects his foe to take advantage of him, he is watchful and quick to suspect trickery. Under such circumstances it is possible to be deceived sometimes and for a short while, but because the victim is resisting, he may break out of the trap and escape before too long.

With the self-deceived it is quite different. He is his own enemy and is working a fraud upon himself. He wants to believe the lie and is psychologically conditioned to do so.

He does not resist the deceit but collaborates with it against himself. There is no struggle, because the victim surrenders before the fight begins. He enjoys being deceived.

It is altogether possible to practice fraud upon our own souls and go deceived to judgment. "If a man think himself to be something, when he is nothing," said Paul, "he deceiveth himself." With this agrees the inspired James: "If any man among you seem to be religious, and bridleth not his tongue, but deceiveth his own heart, this man's religion is vain."

The farther we push into the sanctuary, the greater becomes the danger of self-deception. The deeply religious man is far more vulnerable than the easygoing fellow who takes his religion lightly. This latter may be deceived but he is not likely to be self-deceived.

Under the pressure of deep spiritual concern, and before his heart has been wholly conquered by the Spirit of God, a man may be driven to try every dodge to save face and preserve a semblance of his old independence. This is always dangerous and if persisted in may prove calamitous.

The fallen heart is by nature idolatrous. There appears to be no limit to which some of us will go to save our idol, while at the same time telling ourselves eagerly that we are trusting in Christ alone. It takes a violent act of renunciation to deliver us from the hidden idol, and since very few modern Christians understand that such an act is necessary, and only a small number of those who know are willing to do, it follows that relatively few professors of the Christian faith these days have ever experienced the painful act of renunciation that frees the heart from idolatry.

Prayer is usually recommended as the panacea for all ills and the key to open every prison door, and it would indeed be difficult to overstate the advantages and privilege of Spirit-inspired prayer. But we must not forget that unless we are wise and watchful, prayer itself may become a source of self-deception. There are as many kinds of prayer as there are problems and some kinds are not acceptable to God. The prophets of the Old Testament denounced Israel for trying to hide their iniquities behind their prayers.

Christ flatly rejected the prayers of hypocrites and James declared that some religious persons ask and receive not because they ask amiss.

To escape self-deception the praying man must come out clean and honest. He cannot hide in the cross while concealing in his bosom the golden wedge and the goodly Babylonish garment. Grace will save a man but it will not save him *and* his idol. The blood of Christ will shield the penitent sinner alone, but never the sinner and his idol.

Faith will justify the sinner, but it will never justify the sinner and his sin.

No amount of pleading will make evil good or wrong right. A man may engage in a great deal of humble talk before God and get no response because unknown to himself he is using prayer to disguise disobedience. He may lie for hours in sackcloth and ashes with no higher motive than to try to persuade God to come over on his side so he can have his own way. He may grovel before God in a welter of self-accusation, refuse to give up his secret sin and be rejected for his pains. It can happen.

Dr. H. M. Shuman once said to me in private conversation that he believed the one quality God required a man to have before He would save him was honesty. With this I heartily agree. However dishonest the man may have been before, he must put away his duplicity if he is to be accepted before the Lord. Double dealing is unutterably offensive to God. The insincere man has no claim on mercy. For such a man the cross of Christ provides no remedy. Christ can and will save a man who has been dishonest, but He cannot save him while he is dishonest. Absolute candour is an indispensable requisite to salvation.

How may we remain free from self-deception? The answer sounds old-fashioned and dull but here it is: Mean what you say and never say what you do not mean, either to God or man. Think candid thoughts and act forth-rightly always, whatever the consequence. To do this will bring the cross into your life and keep you dead to self and to public opinion. And it may get you into trouble sometimes, too. But a guileless mind is a great treasure; it is worth any price.

10.Not Attempting to Escape Deception

There are areas of Christian thought, and because of thought then also of life, where likenesses and differences are so difficult to distinguish that we are often hard put to it to escape complete deception.

Throughout the whole world error and truth travel the same highways, work in the same fields and factories, attend the same churches, fly in the same planes and shop in the same stores. So skilled is this error at imitating truth that the two are constantly being mistaken for each. It takes a sharp eye these days to know which brother is Cain and which is Abel.

We must never take for granted anything that touches our soul's welfare. Isaac felt Jacob's arms and thought they were the arms of Esau. Even the disciples failed to spot the traitor among them. The only one of them who knew who he was, was Judas himself. That soft-spoken companion with whom we walk so comfortably and in whose company we take such delight may be an angel of Satan, whereas that rough, plainspoken man whom we shun may be God's very prophet sent to warn us against danger and eternal loss.

It is therefore critically important that the Christian take full advantage of every provision God has made to save him from delusion. These are *prayer, faith, constant meditation on Scripture, obedience, humility, hard, serious thought and the illumination of the Holy Spirit.*

1. *Prayer* is not a surefire protection against error for the reason that there are many kinds of prayer and some of them are worse than useless. The prophets of Baal leaped upon the altar in a frenzy of prayer, but their cries went unregarded because they prayed to a god that did not exist. The God the Pharisees prayed to did exist, but He refused to listen to them because of their self-righteousness and pride. From them we may well learn a profitable lesson in reverse.

In spite of the difficulties we encounter when we pray, prayer is a powerful and effective way to get right, stay right and stay free from error. *"If any of you lack wisdom, let him ask of God, that giveth to all men liberally, and upbraideth not; and it shall be given him."* (James 1:5) All things else being equal, the praying man is less likely to think wrong than the man who neglects to pray. *"Men ought always to pray, and not to faint."* (Luke 18:1)

2. The apostle Paul calls *faith* a shield. The man of faith can walk at ease, protected by his simple confidence in God. God loves to be trusted, and He puts all heaven at the disposal of the trusting soul.

But when we talk of faith let us know what we mean. Faith is not optimism, though it may breed optimism; it is not cheerfulness, though the man of faith is likely to be reasonably cheerful; it is not a vague sense of well-being or a tender appreciation for the beauty of human togetherness. Faith is confidence in God's self-revelation as found in the Holy Scriptures.

3. "Faith cometh by hearing, and hearing by the word of God" (Romans 10:17). *The Scriptures* purify, instruct, strengthen, enlighten and inform. The blessed man will meditate in them day and night.

4. To be entirely safe from the devil's snares the man of God must be completely *obedient to the Word of the Lord.* The driver on the highway is safe, not when he reads the signs but when he obeys them. So it is with the Scriptures. To be effective they must be obeyed.

5. Again, there is a close relation between *humility* and the perception of truth. *"The meek will he guide in judgment: and the meek will he teach his way."* (Psalm 25:9) In the Scriptures I find no shred of encouragement for the proud. Only the tame sheep can be led; only the humble child need expect the guidance of the Father's hand. When all the evidence is in, it may well be found that none but the proud ever strayed from the truth, and that self-trust was behind every heresy that ever afflicted the Church.

6. Then we must *think.* Human thought has its limitations, but where there is no thinking there is not likely to be any large deposit of truth in the mind. Evangelicals at the moment appear to be divided into two camps—those who trust the human intellect to the point of sheer rationalism, and those who are shy of everything intellectual and are convinced that thinking is a waste of the Christian's time.

Surely both are wrong. Self-conscious intellectualism is offensive to man and, I am convinced, to God also, but it is significant that every major revelation in the Scriptures was made to a man of superior intellect. It would be easy to marshal an imposing list of biblical quotations exhorting us to think, but a more convincing argument is the whole drift of the Bible itself. The Scriptures simply take for granted that the saints of the Most High will be serious-minded, thoughtful persons. They never leave the impression that it is sinful to think.

7. But thinking apart from the *inward illumination of the Holy Spirit* is not only futile, it is likely to be dangerous as well. The human intellect is fallen and can no more find its way through the broad expanse of truth, half-truth and downright error than a ship can find its way over the ocean alone. God has given us the Holy Spirit to illuminate our minds. He is eyes and understanding to us. We dare not try to get on without Him.

11.Artificial Preaching

When I was a young lad and first beginning to observe the human scene, one thing that struck me forcibly was the artificiality of preachers. The world they inhabited was, it seemed to me, always once removed from reality.

I was not brought up in a Christian home and so was not accustomed to the conventional language of religion, and when I chanced occasionally to hear a sermon I listened with an ear undulled by familiarity. How strange the preachers sounded to me, how artificial their tones and how unnatural their demeanor.

They were men, obviously, but they lacked completely the candor and downrightness I knew so well in other men. The bold, man-to-man approach was missing. They seemed to be afraid of something, though I could not tell what, for certainly the tame, patient, almost indifferent persons who listened to them were harmless enough. No one paid much attention to what they said anyway. I am sure that if one of them had slyly interspersed into his sermon stray bits of the Gettysburg Address repeated backward few of those present would have noticed or cared. Yet they spoke so gingerly and apologetically that one got the impression that they would rather remain silent forever than to offend anyone. After listening to some of them now and again, I knew the meaning of the French saying (though I did not hear it till many years later), "There are three sexes: men, women and preachers."

Now I am all for preachers and I do not expect them to be perfect, but I am all for downrightness, too. I think it highly improbable that anyone who speaks cautiously can speak effectively. His timidity will deactivate his effort and render it impotent.

It is true that the church has suffered from pugnacious men who would rather fight than pray, but she has suffered more from timid preachers who would rather be nice than be right. The latter have done more harm if for no other reason than that there are so many more of them. I do not think, however, that we must make our choice between the two. It is altogether possible to have love and courage at the same time, to be both true and faithful. *"Let your speech be alway with grace, seasoned with salt.*" (Colossians 4:6) It is the absence of salt that makes so much of our preaching vapid and dull. *"Can that which is unsavoury be eaten without salt? or is there any taste in the white of an egg?"* (Job 6:6)

Our theological schools may be at fault here. They strive to turn out preachers who will be all things to all men, in a sense Paul never had in mind. They want their students to be cultured if it kills them, and they begin by draining off all salt and leaving only a sweetness and light that appears to some of us to be neither sweet nor light.

Everything natural is as far as possible refined away. All tang is eliminated from the speech, all angularity carefully filed off the language. The young man is trained to gesture gracefully, smile faintly and sound scholarly. The direct language that men naturally use when speaking to each other is edited out and a vague, stilted jargon is substituted for it. The total result is artificiality and ineffectiveness.

But back to my own experience: it was by the mercy of God that I was later permitted to hear an evangelist who was completely human and paid his hearers the compliment of assuming that they were human too. He knew what he wanted to say and said it fearlessly; and the people knew what he meant and either took it or left it. Thank God a good number of them took it.

Every man who stands to proclaim the Word should speak with something of the bold authority of the Word itself. The Bible is the book of supreme love, but it is at the same time altogether frank and downright. Its writers are never rude or unkind, but they are invariably honest and entirely sincere. A great sense of urgency is upon everything they write. They are deeply concerned with moral decisions. Protocol is of less interest to them than the glory of God and the welfare of the people.

One is tempted to offer advice to the young preacher to prevent him from becoming a mere purveyor of artificial religious platitudes, but further consideration shows how useless that would be. One might urge him to study the best writers and speakers, to strive to be original, to look at and through things before speaking of them, to avoid cliches, to speak in the vernacular; but this is to miss the point entirely.

Religious artificiality is not a technical thing but a deeply human and spiritual one. It is a disease of the soul and can only be healed by the

Physician of souls.

To escape the snare of artificiality, it is necessary that a man enjoy a satisfying personal experience with God. He must be totally committed to Christ and deeply anointed with the Holy Spirit. Further, he must be delivered from the fear of man. The focus of his attention must be God and not men. He must let everything dear to him ride out on each sermon. He must so preach as to jeopardize his future, his ministry, even his life itself. He must make God responsible for the consequences and speak as one who will not have long to speak before he is called to judgment. Then the people will know they are hearing a voice instead of a mere echo.

12.Misunderstanding Freedom

Freedom is priceless. Where it is present almost any kind of life is enjoyable. When it is absent life can never be enjoyed; it can only be endured.

Millions have died in freedom's defense and her praise is in everyone's mouth. Yet, she has been tragically misunderstood by her advocates and sorely wounded in the house of her friends. I think the difficulty lies with our failure to distinguish freedom from liberty, which are indeed sisters but not identical twins.

Freedom is liberty within bounds: liberty to obey holy laws, liberty to keep the commandments of Christ, to serve mankind, to develop to the full all the latent possibilities within our redeemed natures. True Christian liberty never sets us free to indulge our lusts or to follow our fallen impulses.

The desire for unqualified freedom caused the fall of Lucifer and wrought the destruction of the angels that sinned. They sought freedom to do as they willed, and to get it they threw away the beautiful liberty that meant freedom to do the will of God. And the human race followed them in their tragic moral blunder.

To anyone who bothers to think a bit, it should be evident that there is in the universe no such thing as absolute freedom. Only God is free. It is inherent in creaturehood that its freedom must be limited by the will of the Creator and the nature of the thing created. The glory of heaven lies in the character of the freedom enjoyed by those who dwell therein.

That innumerable company of angels, the general assembly and Church of the First-born and the spirits of just men made perfect are at liberty to fulfill all the broad purposes of God. This liberty secures for them an infinitely greater degree of happiness than unqualified freedom could do.

Unqualified freedom in any area of human life is deadly. In government it is anarchy, in domestic life free love and in religion antinomianism. The freest cells in the body are cancer cells, but they kill the organism where they grow. A healthy society requires that its members accept a limited freedom. Each must curtail his own liberty that all may be free, and this law runs throughout all the created universe, including the kingdom of God.

Too much liberty weakens whatever it touches. The corn of wheat can bring forth fruit only as it waives its freedom and surrenders itself to the laws of nature. The robin may fly about all summer enjoying her freedom, but if she wants a nest full of fledglings, she must sit as a voluntary captive for weeks while the mystery of life gestates beneath her soft feathers. She has her choice: be free and barren or curtail her freedom and bring forth young.

Every man in a free society must decide whether he will exploit his liberty or curtail it for intelligent and moral ends. He may take upon him the responsibility of a business and a family and thus be useful to the race, or he may shun all obligations and end on skid row. The tramp is freer than president or king, but his freedom is his undoing. While he lives, he remains socially sterile, and when he dies, he leaves behind him nothing to make the world glad he lived.

The Christian cannot escape the peril of too much liberty. He is indeed free, but his very freedom may prove a source of real temptation to him. He is free from the chains of sin, free from the moral consequences of evil acts now forgiven, free from the curse of the law and the displeasure of God. Grace has opened the prison door for him, and like Barabbas of old he walks at liberty because Another died in his stead.

All this the instructed Christian knows and he refuses to let false teachers and misguided religionists rivet a yoke of bondage upon his neck. But now what shall he do with his freedom?

Two possibilities offer themselves. He may accept his blood-won freedom as a cloak for the flesh, as the New Testament declares that some have done, or he may kneel like the camel to receive his voluntary burden.

And what is this burden? The woes of his fellowmen which he must do what he can to assuage; the debt which he along with Paul owes to the lost world; the sound of hungry children crying in the night; the church in Babylonian captivity; the swift onrush of evil doctrines and the success of false prophets; the slow decay of the moral foundations of the so-called Christian nations, and whatever else demands self-sacrifice, cross-carrying, long prayer vigils and courageous witness to alleviate and correct.

Christianity is the religion of freedom and democracy is freedom in organized society, but if we continue to misunderstand this freedom, we may soon have neither Christianity nor democracy. To protect political liberty free men must lay a voluntary obligation upon themselves; to preserve the religion of salvation by free grace a great many Christians must waive their right to be free and take upon themselves a load greater than they have ever carried before.

When the state is in danger, it can conscript men to fight for her freedom, but there are no conscripts in the army of the Lord. To bear a cross the Christian must take it up of his own free will. No authority can compel us to feed the hungry or evangelize the lost or pray for revival or sacrifice ourselves for Christ's sake and the sake of suffering humanity.

The ideal Christian is one who knows he is free to do as he will and wills to be a servant. This is the path Christ took; blessed is the man who follows Him.

13.Conformity

A stimulating little book written by a thoughtful observer of the religious scene attempts to explain Christian sects and denominations as reflections of the social conditions out of which they sprang.

The idea is, if I understand the author's arguments correctly, that differences in doctrine and in forms of church government among various Christian bodies have resulted from different economic, political, racial and cultural patterns throughout Christendom.

According to this theory, a democratic state would tend to produce a democratic church, whereas under a political dictatorship the authoritarian form of government would naturally prevail within the Christian community. In a highly cultured society, ritualism would mark the worship of the church, along with much rich symbolism and forms of external beauty.

I am not ready to say whether this conforms to historic fact, though my limited knowledge of history would lead me to believe that this explanation is probably an accommodation of fact to theory and, while partly true, does not tell the whole story. One thing is certain, however. It is that wherever the Christian religion differs from itself, there will surely be found elements that are unscriptural and altogether without biblical authority, and it is always those elements that divide the church against itself.

In whatever language they appear, the Scriptures continue century after century to say the same thing to everyone. The Spirit that inspired the Christian revelation never differs from Himself, but remains from age to age the same. God works according to an eternal purpose which He purposed in Christ Jesus before the world began, and our Lord assures us that till heaven and earth pass, one jot or one tittle shall in no wise pass from the Law till all be fulfilled. God's truth is the same wherever it is found and if the church conforms to the truth, it will be the same church in doctrine and in practice throughout the entire world.

There are in the Christian religion three major elements: spiritual life, moral practice and community organization, and these all spring out of and follow New Testament doctrine; or more correctly, the first must and the others should. Life is and must necessarily be first. Life comes mysteriously to the soul that believes the truth.

"He that heareth my word, and believeth on him that sent me, hath everlasting life, and shall not come into condemnation; but is passed from death unto life." (John 5:24)

And again,

He that believeth on me, as the scripture hath said, out of his belly shall flow rivers of living water. (But this spake he of the Spirit, which they that believe on him should receive: for the Holy Ghost was not yet given; because that Jesus was not yet glorified). (7:38–39)

The message of the cross offers eternal life and the blessedness of the Holy Spirit indwelling the soul. These distinguish Christianity from every other religion, and it is significant that these distinguishing marks are of such a nature as to be wholly above and beyond the reach of man. They are altogether mysterious and divine and are unaffected by race, politics, economics or education. The life of God in the soul of a man is wholly independent of the social status of that man. In the early church, the Spirit leaped across all artificial lines that separate men from each other and made of all believers a spiritual brotherhood. Jew and Gentile, rich and poor, Greek and barbarian were all baptized into one body, of which Christ was and is the Head.

Along with the gift of eternal life, the entrance of the Holy Spirit into the believer's heart and the induction of the newborn soul into the Body of Christ comes instant obligation to obey the teachings of the New Testament.

These teachings are so plain and so detailed that it is difficult to understand how they could appear different to persons living under different political systems or on different cultural levels. That they have so appeared cannot be denied; but always the reasons lie in the imperfect state of the believers composing the different groups. They permitted the unauthorized introduction of extrascriptural matter into their beliefs and suffered spiritual weakness and debility as a consequence.

Undoubtedly Christian groups have been influenced in their moral practices by the society in which they lived, but we should see it for what it is and not try to explain it away. *"Whosoever therefore shall break one of these least commandments, and shall teach men so, he shall be called the least in the kingdom of heaven."* (Matthew 5:19)

That we Christians modify the moral teachings of Christ at our convenience in order to avoid the stigma of being thought different is a proof of our backsliding. The shame of it will not be removed until we have repented and brought our lives completely under the discipline of Christ.

The third element in the Christian religion, that of church polity or the political organization of the religious community in worship and service, is subject to the pressures and influences of society to a greater degree than are the other two.

A modern example of this is the Salvation Army, which is to all intents and purposes a Christian denomination imitating the military in its organization and nomenclature. Other examples may be found in the historic denominations which have often followed rather closely the organization of the state. That some may deny this and quote Scripture to justify their organizational pattern does not invalidate my statement.

Christianity does vary from itself from place to place and from time to time, as it permits itself to be influenced by political, economic, racial or cultural factors. Without doubt neither I who write this nor you who read it can be said to have escaped completely the molding power of society. As Christians we are somewhat different from what we would have been had we lived in a different period of history.

I think we do well to admit this, but we should not accept it as normal; and certainly we should not accept it as inevitable that we continue to be shaped by the world. Paul said, *"And be not conformed to this world: but be ye transformed by the renewing of your mind."* (Romans 12:2)

That we have to some extent conformed to the world is a proof of our weakness. We must begin at once to correct matters. By consecration, detachment, obedience and unceasing prayer we must escape the clutches of the world. Pure Christianity, instead of being shaped by its environment, actually stands in sharp opposition to it, and where the power of God has been present over a sustained period, the church has sometimes reversed the direction of things and exercised a purifying effect upon society.

14.Loving Wrong

"To be another than I am I must abandon that I am."—Chrysostom

We are all in process of becoming. We have already moved from what we were to what we are, and we are now moving toward what we shall be.

That our character is not solid but fluid is not in itself a disturbing thought. Indeed, the man who knows himself may take great comfort in the realization that he is not fixed in his present state. He may cease to be what he is ashamed that he has ever been, and he can go on to be "remolded nearer to the heart's desire."

The perturbing thought is not that we are becoming, but what we are becoming; not that we are moving, but toward what we are moving. For it is not in human nature to move on a horizontal plane; we are either ascending or descending, mounting up or sinking down. When a moral being travels from one to another position, it must always be toward the worse or toward the better.

This corresponds to a spiritual law revealed in the Revelation. *"He that is unjust, let him be unjust still: and he which is filthy, let him be filthy still: and he that is righteous, let him be righteous still: and he that is holy, let him be holy still."* (Revelation 22:11)

Not only are we all in the process of becoming, we are becoming what we love. We are, to a large degree, the sum of our loves, and we will of moral necessity grow into the image of what we love most. For love is among other things a creative affinity; it changes and molds and shapes and transforms. It is without doubt the most powerful agent affecting human nature next to the direct action of the Holy Spirit of God within the soul.

What we love is therefore not a small matter to be lightly shrugged off. Rather, it is of present, critical and everlasting importance. It is prophetic of our future. It tells us what we shall be, and so predicts accurately our eternal destiny.

Loving wrong objects is fatal to spiritual growth; it twists and deforms the life and makes impossible the appearing of the image of

Christ in the soul. It is only as we love right objects that we become right, and only as we go on loving them that we continue to experience a slow but continuous transmutation toward the objects of our purified affection.

This furnishes in part (but only in part) a rational explanation for the first and greatest commandment: *"Thou shalt love the Lord thy God with all thy heart, and with all thy soul, and with all thy mind."* (Matthew 22:37)   .

To become like God is and must be the supreme goal of all moral creatures. This is the reason for their creation, the end apart from which no excuse can be found for their existence. Leaving out of consideration for the moment those strange and beautiful heavenly beings of which we have hints in the Bible but about which we know so little, we concentrate upon the fallen race of mankind. Once made in the image of God we kept not our first estate, but left our proper habitation, consorted with Satan and walked according to the course of this world, according to the prince of the power of the air, the spirit that now worketh in the children of disobedience: But God, who is rich in mercy, for his great love wherewith he loved us, even when we were dead in sins, hath quickened us together with Christ. (Ephesians 2:2–5)

The supreme work of Christ in redemption is not to save us from hell but to restore us to Godlikeness again, the purpose being stated in Romans: *"For whom he did foreknow, he also did predestinate to be conformed to the image of his Son."* (Romans 8:29)

While perfect restoration to the divine image awaits the day of Christ's appearing, the work of restoration is now going on. There is a slow but steady transmutation of the base metal of human nature into the gold of Godlikeness effected by the faith-filled gaze of the soul at the glory of God in the face of Jesus Christ (2 Corinthians 3:18).

Right here we might do well to anticipate a difficulty and try to clear it away, a difficulty that arises from an erroneous conception of love. The problem may be stated this way: Love is whimsical, unpredictable and almost wholly beyond our control. It springs up and burns on or dies of itself. How then can we control our love? How can we direct it toward worthy objects? And particularly, how can we force it to rest on God as the proper and permanent object of its devotion?

Were love indeed unpredictable and beyond our control, these questions could have no satisfactory answers and our outlook would be hopeless. The simple truth is, however, that spiritual love is not the capricious and irresponsible emotion men mistakenly believe it to be. It is the servant of the will and must ever go where it is sent and do what it is told.

The romantic phrase "fall in love" has given people the notion that we are perforce victims of the arrows of Cupid and can have no control over our affections. The average young person these days expects to fall in love after the love-in-idleness pattern of Oberon and Titania and be swept away by a tempest of delightful emotions. Unconsciously we extend this concept of love to our relation to our Creator and ask, how can we make ourselves love God supremely?

The answer to this and all related questions is that the love we have for God is not the love of feeling, but the love of willing. Love is within our power of choice, otherwise we would not be commanded to love God nor be held accountable for not loving Him.

The taking over of the romantic love ideal into our relation to God has been extremely injurious to our Christian lives. The idea that we should "fall in love" with God is ignoble, unscriptural, unworthy of us, and certainly does no honor to the Most High God.

We do not come to love God by a sudden emotional visitation. Love for God results from repentance, amendment of life and a fixed determination to love Him. As God moves more perfectly into the focus of our hearts, our love for Him may indeed rise and swell within us till like a flood it sweeps everything before it.

But we should not wait for this intensity of feeling. We are not responsible to feel but we are responsible to love, and true spiritual love begins in the will. We should set our hearts to love God supremely, however cold or hard they may seem to be, and go on to confirm our love by careful and happy obedience to His Word. Enjoyable emotions are sure to follow. Bird song and blossoms do not make the spring, but when the spring comes, they come with it.

Now I would hasten to disclaim all sympathy with the popular salvation-by-willpower cult. I am in radical disagreement with all forms of quasi-Christianity that depend upon the "latent power within us" or trust to "creative thinking" instead of to the power of God. All these paper-thin religious philosophies break down at the same place—in the erroneous assumption that the stream of human nature can be made to run backward up over the falls. This it can never do. "Salvation is of the Lord."

To be saved a lost man must be picked up bodily by the power of God and raised to a higher level. There must be an impartation of divine life in the wonder of the second birth before the words of the apostle apply to him: *"But we all, with open face beholding as in a glass the glory of the Lord, are changed into the same image from glory to glory, even as by the Spirit of the Lord."* (2 Corinthians 3:18)

It has been established here, I hope, that human nature is in a formative state and that it is being changed into the image of the thing it loves. Men and women are being molded by their affinities, shaped by their affections and powerfully transformed by the artistry of their loves. In the unregenerate world of Adam, this produces day-by-day tragedies of cosmic proportions.

Think of the power that turned an innocent pink-cheeked boy into a Nero or a Himmler. And was Jezebel always the "cursed woman" whose head and hands the very dogs, with poetic justice, refused to eat? No; once she dreamed her pure girlish dreams and blushed at the thoughts of womanly love; but soon she became interested in evil things, admired them and went on at last to love them. There the law of moral affinity took over, and Jezebel, like clay in the hand of the potter, was turned to the deformed and hateful thing that the chamberlains threw down from the window.

For His own children, our heavenly Father has provided right moral objects for admiration and love. These are to God as the colors in the rainbow round about the throne. They are not God but they are nearest to God; we cannot love Him without loving them, and as we love them, we are enabled to love Him more. What are they?

The first is *righteousness*. Our Lord Jesus loved righteousness and hated iniquity (Hebrews 1:9), and for this reason God anointed Him with the oil of gladness above His fellows. Here the pattern is fixed. To love is also to hate. The heart that is drawn to righteousness will be repulsed by iniquity in the same degree, and this moral repulsion is hate. The holiest man is the one who loves righteousness most and hates evil with the most perfect hatred.

The next is *wisdom*. From the Greeks we take the word "philosophy," the love of wisdom, but before the Greek philosophers were the Hebrew prophets and their concept of wisdom was loftier and more spiritual than anything known in Greece. The wisdom literature of the Old Testament—Proverbs, Ecclesiastes (and to some degree the Psalms)—breathes with a love of wisdom unknown even to Plato.

So high do the Old Testament writers place wisdom that sometimes we can scarcely distinguish the wisdom that comes from God from the wisdom that is God. The Hebrews anticipated by some centuries the Greek idea of God as essential wisdom, though their concept of wisdom was less intellectual than moral. To them the wise man was the good man, the godly man, and wisdom at its noblest reaches was to love God and keep His commandments.

The Hebrew thinker could not divorce wisdom from righteousness. Two of the greatest of the apocryphal books, Wisdom of Solomon and Ecclesiasticus, celebrate the wisdom that consorts with righteousness with an eloquence that is sometimes equal to that of the canonical Scriptures.

Another object for Christian love to fix upon is *truth*, and again we have difficulty separating the truth of God from God Himself. Christ said, "I am the truth," and in so saying joined truth and the Deity in inseparable union. To love God is to love truth, and to love truth with steadfast ardor is to grow toward the image of truth and away from the lie and the error.

It is unnecessary to name or try to name all the other good and holy things God has approved as our models. The Bible sets them before us—mercy, kindness, purity, humility and many more, and the Spirit-taught souls will know what to do about them.

The sum of it all seems to be that we should cultivate interest in and love for the morally beautiful. Was that why Paul wrote to the Philippians (Philippians 4:8): "*Finally, brethren, whatsoever things are true, whatsoever things are honest, whatsoever things are just, whatsoever things are pure, whatsoever things are lovely, whatsoever things are of good report; if there be any virtue, and if there be any praise, think on these things*"?

15. A Playground Attitude

Things are for us not only what they are. They are what we hold them to be. Which is to say that our attitude toward things is likely in the long run to be more important than the things themselves.

This is a common coin of knowledge, like an old dime, worn smooth by use. Yet it bears upon it the stamp of truth and must not be rejected because it is familiar.

It is strange how a fact may remain fixed, while our interpretation of the fact changes with the generations and the years.

One such fact is the world in which we live. It is here, and has been here through the centuries. It is a stable fact, quite unchanged by the passing of time, but how different is modern man's view of it from the view our fathers held. Here we see plainly how great is the power of interpretation. The world is for all of us not only what it is; it is what we believe it to be. And a tremendous load of woe or weal rides on the soundness of our interpretation.

We are able to see the wide gulf between our modern attitudes and those of our fathers by going no further back than the times of the founding and early development of our country.

In the early days, when Christianity exercised a dominant influence over American thinking, men conceived the world to be a battle-ground. Our fathers believed in sin and the devil and hell as constituting one force; and they believed in God and righteousness and heaven as the other. These were opposed to each other in the nature of them forever in deep, grave, irreconcilable hostility.

Man, so our fathers held, had to choose sides; he could not be neutral. For him it must be life or death, heaven or hell, and if he chose to come out on God's side, he could expect open war with God's enemies. The fight would be real and deadly and would last as long as life continued here below. Men looked forward to heaven as a return from the wars, a laying down of the sword to enjoy in peace the home prepared for them.

Sermons and songs in those days often had a martial quality about them, or perhaps a trace of homesickness. The Christian soldier thought of home and rest and reunion, and his voice grew plaintive as he sang of battle ended and victory won. But whether he was charging into enemy guns or dreaming of war's end and the Father's welcome home, he never forgot what kind of world he lived in. It was a battleground, and many were the wounded and the slain.

That view of things is unquestionably the scriptural one. Allowing for the figures and metaphors with which the Scriptures abound, it still is a solid Bible doctrine that tremendous spiritual forces are present in the world, and man, because of his spiritual nature, is caught in the middle. The evil powers are bent upon destroying him, while Christ is present to save him through the power of the gospel. To obtain deliverance he must come out on God's side in faith and obedience. That in brief is what our fathers thought; and that, we believe, is what the Bible teaches.

How different it is today. The fact remains the same, but the interpretation has changed completely. Men think of the world not as a battleground but as a playground. We are not here to fight; we are here to frolic. We are not in a foreign land; we are at home. We are not getting ready to live, we are already living, and the best we can do is to rid ourselves of our inhibitions and our frustrations and live this life to the full.

This, we believe, is a fair summary of the religious philosophy of modern man, openly professed by millions and tacitly held by more multiplied millions who live out that philosophy without having given verbal expression to it.

This changed attitude toward the world has had and is having its effect upon Christians, even gospel Christians who profess the faith of the Bible. By a curious juggling of the figures, they manage to add up the column wrong and yet claim to have the right answer. It sounds fantastic but it is true.

That this world is a playground instead of a battleground has now been accepted in practice by the vast majority of evangelical Christians. They might hedge around the question if they were asked bluntly to declare their position, but their conduct gives them away. They are facing both ways, enjoying Christ and the world too, and gleefully telling everyone that accepting Jesus does not require them to give up their fun, and that Christianity is just the jolliest thing imaginable.

The "worship" growing out of such a view of life is as far off center as the view itself, a sort of sanctified nightclubbing without the champagne and the dressed-up drunks.

This whole thing has grown to be so serious of late that it now becomes the bounden duty of every Christian to reexamine his spiritual philosophy in the light of the Bible, and having discovered the scriptural way to follow it, even if to do so he must separate himself from much that he formerly accepted as real but which now in the light of truth he knows to be false.

A right view of God and the world to come requires that we have also a right view of the world in which we live and our relation to it. So much depends upon this that we cannot afford to be careless about it.

16. The Worship of Eros

The period in which we now live may well go down in history as the Erotic Age. Sex love has been elevated into a cult. Eros has more worshipers among civilized men today than any other god. For millions, the erotic has completely displaced the spiritual.

How the world got into this state is not difficult to trace. Contributing factors are the phonograph and radio, which can spread a love song from coast to coast within a matter of days; the motion picture and television, which enable a whole population to feast their eyes on sensuous women and amorous young men locked in passionate embrace (and this in the living rooms of "Christian" homes and before the eyes of innocent children!); shorter working hours and a multiplicity of mechanical gadgets with the resultant increased leisure for everyone.

Add to these the scores of shrewdly contrived advertising campaigns, which make sex the not too slyly concealed bait to attract buyers for almost every imaginable product; the degraded columnists who have consecrated their lives to the task of the publicizing of soft, slinky nobodies with the faces of angels and the morals of alley cats; conscienceless novelists who win a doubtful fame and grow rich at the inglorious chore of dredging up literary putridities from the sewers of their souls to provide entertainment for the masses.

These tell us something about how Eros has achieved his triumph over the civilized world.

Now if this god would let us Christians alone, I for one would let his cult alone. The whole spongy, fetid mess will sink some day under its own weight, and become excellent fuel for the fires of hell—this would be just recompense, and it becomes us to feel compassion for those who have been caught in its tragic collapse. Tears and silence might be better than words, if things were slightly otherwise than they are.

But the cult of Eros is seriously affecting the Church. The pure religion of Christ that flows like a crystal river from the heart of God is being polluted by the unclean waters that trickle from behind the altars of abomination that appear on every high hill and under every green tree from New York to Los Angeles.

The influence of the erotic spirit is felt almost everywhere in evangelical circles. Much of the singing in certain types of meetings has in it more of romance than it has of the Holy Ghost. Both words and music are designed to rouse the libidinous. Christ is courted with a familiarity that reveals a total ignorance of who He is. It is not the reverent intimacy of the adoring saint but the impudent familiarity of the carnal lover.

Religious fiction also makes use of sex to interest the reading public. The paper-thin excuse is that, if romance and religion are woven into a story, the average person who would not read a purely religious book will read the story and thus be exposed to the gospel.

Leaving aside the fact that most modern religious novelists are home talent amateurs, scarcely one of whom is capable of writing a single line of even fair literature, the whole concept behind the religio-romantic novel is unsound. The libidinous impulses and the sweet, deep movings of the Holy Spirit are diametrically opposed to each other.

The notion that Eros can be made to serve as an assistant of the Lord of glory is outrageous. The "Christian" film that seeks to draw customers by picturing amorous love scenes in its advertising is completely false to the religion of Christ. Only the spiritually blind will be taken in by it.

The current vogue of physical beauty and sparkling personalities in religious promotion is a further manifestation of the influence of the romantic spirit in the Church. The rhythmic sway, the synthetic smile, and the too, *too* cheerful voice betray the religious worldling. He has learned his technique from the TV screen, but not learned it well enough to succeed in the professional field. So, he brings his inept production to the holy place, and peddles it to the ailing and undersized Christians who are looking for something to amuse them while staying within the bounds of the current religious mores.

If my language should seem severe, let it be remembered that it is not directed at any individual. Toward the lost world of men, I feel only a great compassion and a desire that all should come to repentance. For the Christians, whose vigorous but mistaken leadership has wooed the modern church from the altar of Jehovah to the altars of error, I feel genuine love and sympathy. I want to be the last to injure them and the first to forgive them, remembering my past sins and my need for mercy, as well as my own weakness and natural bent toward sin and error.

Balaam's ass was used of God to rebuke a prophet. It would seem from this that God does not require perfection in the instrument He uses to warn and exhort His people.

When God's sheep are in danger the shepherd must not gaze at the stars and meditate on "inspirational" themes. He is morally obliged to grab his weapon and run to their defense. When the circumstances call for it, love can use the sword, though by her nature she would rather bind up the broken heart and minister to the wounded. It is time for the prophet and the seer to make themselves heard and felt again. For the last three decades timidity disguised as humility has crouched in her corner while the spiritual quality of evangelical Christianity has become progressively worse year by year.

How long, O Lord, how long?

17.Attachment to Entertainment

A German philosopher many years ago said something to the effect that the more a man has in his own heart the less he will require from the outside; excessive need for support from without is proof of the bankruptcy of the inner man.

If this is true (and I believe it is), then the present inordinate attachment to every form of entertainment is evidence that the inner life of modern man is in serious decline. The average man has no central core of moral assurance, no spring within his own breast, no inner strength to place him above the need for repeated psychological shots to give him the courage to go on living. He has become a parasite on the world, drawing his life from his environment, unable to live a day apart from the stimulation which society affords him.

Schleiermacher held that the feeling of dependence lies at the root of all religious worship, and that however high the spiritual life might rise, it must always begin with a deep sense of a great need which only God could satisfy. If this sense of need and a feeling of dependence are at the root of natural religion, it is not hard to see why the great god Entertainment is so ardently worshiped by so many. For there are millions who cannot live without amusement; life without some form of entertainment for them is simply intolerable; they look forward to the blessed relief afforded by professional entertainers and other forms of psychological narcotics as a dope addict looks to his daily shot of heroin. Without them they could not summon the courage to face existence.

No one with common human feeling will object to the simple pleasures of life, nor to such harmless forms of entertainment as may help to relax the nerves and refresh the mind exhausted by toil. Such things, if used with discretion, may be a blessing along the way. That is one thing. The all-out devotion to entertainment as a major activity for which and by which men live is definitely something else again.

The abuse of a harmless thing is the essence of sin. The growth of the amusement phase of human life to such fantastic proportions is a portent, a threat to the souls of modern man. It has been built into a multimillion-dollar racket with greater power over human minds and human character than any other educational influence on earth. And the ominous thing is that its power is almost exclusively evil, rotting the inner life, crowding out the long eternal thoughts which would fill the souls of men if they were but worthy to entertain them. And the whole thing has grown into a veritable religion which holds its devotees with a strange fascination, and a religion, incidentally, against which it is now dangerous to speak.

For centuries the Church stood solidly against every form of worldly entertainment, recognizing it for what it was—a device for wasting time, a refuge from the disturbing voice of conscience, a scheme to divert attention from moral accountability. For this she got herself abused roundly by the sons of this world.

But of late she has become tired of the abuse and has gotten over the struggle. She appears to have decided that if she cannot conquer the great god Entertainment she may as well join forces with him and make what use she can of his powers.

So today we have the astonishing spectacle of millions of dollars being poured into the unholy job of providing earthly entertainment for the so-called sons of heaven. Religious entertainment is in many places rapidly crowding out the serious things of God. Many churches these days have become little more than poor theaters where fifth-rate "producers" peddle their shoddy wares with the full approval of evangelical leaders who can even quote a holy text in defense of their delinquency. And hardly a man dares raise his voice against it.

The great god Entertainment amuses his devotees mainly by telling them stories. The love of stories, which is a characteristic of childhood, has taken fast hold of the minds of the retarded saints of our day, so much so that not a few persons manage to make a comfortable living by spinning yarns and serving them up in various disguises to church people. What is natural and beautiful in a child may be shocking when it persists into adulthood, and more so when it appears in the sanctuary and seeks to pass for true religion.

Is it not a strange thing and a wonder that, with the shadow of atomic destruction hanging over the world and with the coming of Christ drawing near, the professed followers of the Lord should be giving themselves up to religious amusements? That in an hour when mature saints are so desperately needed vast numbers of believers should revert to spiritual childhood and clamor for religious toys?

"Remember, O LORD, what is come upon us: consider, and behold our reproach. ... The crown is fallen from our head: woe unto us, that we have sinned! For this our heart is faint; for these things our eyes are dim." (Lamentations 5:1, 16–17) Amen. Amen.

18.Ignorance of the 'Deeper Life'

"Certainly, not all of the mystery of the Godhead can be known by man. But, just as certainly, all that man can know of God in this life is revealed in Jesus Christ!"

Some Christian believers seemingly are committed to endless dialogue about the deeper life just as though it were some new kind of fun and games.

I almost shrink from hearing the expression, "the deeper life," because so many people want to talk about it as a topic—but no one seems to want to know and love God for Himself!

God is the deeper life! Jesus Christ Himself is the deeper life, and as I plunge on into the knowledge of the triune God, my heart moves on into the blessedness of His fellowship. This means that there is less of me and more of God—thus my spiritual life deepens, and I am strengthened in the knowledge of His will.

I think this is what Paul meant when he penned that great desire, "That I may know Him!" (Philippians 3:10). He was expressing more than the desire for acquaintance—he was yearning to be drawn into the full knowledge of fellowship with God which has been provided in the plan of redemption.

God originally created man in His own image so that man could know companionship with God in a unique sense, and to a degree that is impossible for any other creature to experience.

Because of his sin, man lost this knowledge, this daily partnership with God. In the first chapter of Romans, Paul gives us a vivid picture of men and women whom God gave over to a reprobate mind because they did not wish to retain God in their knowledge, their foolish hearts being darkened (see 1:21, 28).

This is the Bible portrait of man. He has that great potential of knowing God as no other creature can, but he is lost. Without God in his knowledge, his conduct is unworthy of his high origin and his being despairs in its encompassing emptiness.

This despair, this emptiness and lostness, reflects man's great problem, because he is an intelligent, moral creature who has left his proper sphere and estate of environment. He is not fulfilling the great end for which he was created as he is a sinner. How can he know anything but endless defeat and pain?

We believe that God created all living creatures, each with its own peculiar kind of life. In each case God adjusted that life to its own environment. Therefore, as long as each living creature remains in its own environment and lives the kind of life for which it was created, it fulfills the purpose for which it was made. Thus, the highest that can be said of any creature is that it fulfilled the purpose for which God made it.

According to the Scriptures, only man was created in God's own image. I can find no reference in the Bible to indicate that God made the seraphim or cherubim, angels or archangels in His own image.

I know that I take a chance of being misunderstood and perhaps of being misjudged when I state that man was more like God than any other creature ever created. Because of the nature of man's creation, there is nothing in the universe so much like God as the human soul. Even in the face of man's sin and lost condition, there is still that basic potential in the soul and nature of man that, through grace, can become more like God than anything in the universe.

There is no question about man's sin—therefore, there is no question about his being lost. A man is lost if he is not converted—overwhelmed in the vast darkness of emptiness. He was created to know God, but he chose the gutter. That is why he is like a bird shut away in a cage or like a fish taken from the water. That is the explanation of man's disgraceful acts—war and hate, murder and greed, brother against brother!

Once the smart men told us that science and philosophy and psychiatry and sociology would soon make the world a better place in which to live. As time passes, however, men are at one another's throats as never before and there is the greatest volume of hate, suspicion, anarchy, treachery, espionage, murder and criminal acts of all kinds in the history of the world.

Is there still a good word for man in his lost condition? Is there an answer for man in whom there is that instinctive groping and craving for the lost image and the knowledge of the Eternal Being?

Yes, there is a positive answer found in the Word of God, and it teaches the sinner-man that it is still possible for him to know God. The Bible teaches us that God has not abandoned the human race as He abandoned the angels who sinned and gave up their first estate.

Studying the Word of God, we must come to the conclusion that God abandoned the sinning angels because they had not been created in the image of God. They were moral creatures, capable of moral and spiritual perception, but they were not made in God's image.

And why has God given sinful man another opportunity in salvation through the merits of a Redeemer? Only because he was made in the image of God, and God has expressed His own everlasting love for man through the giving of His Son.

Now, the Bible has a great deal to say about the manner in which sinful man may come into the fellowship and the presence of God, and it all has to do with forgiveness and grace and regeneration and justification in Jesus Christ! It all boils down to the teaching that Jesus Christ is everything that the Godhead is! The image of the invisible God (Colossians 1:15), the brightness of His glory, the express image of His person (Hebrews 1:3)—all of these we find in and through Jesus Christ!

We believe with rejoicing that Jesus Christ was the begotten of the Father (John 1:14), before all ages (John 1:1), that He is God of God, Light of light, very God of very God, begotten and not made, of one substance with the Father, and it is by Him that all things were made! (see Colossians 1:16).

Nature of the 'Deeper Life'

I advise you not to listen to those who spend their time demeaning the person of Christ. I advise you to look beyond the cloudiness of modern terms used by those who themselves are not sure who Jesus Christ was, in reality.

You cannot trust the man who can only say, "I believe that God revealed Himself through Christ!" Find out what he really believes about the person of the incarnate Son of God!

You cannot trust the man who will only say that Christ reflected more of God than other men do. Neither can you trust those who teach that Jesus Christ was the supreme religious genius, having the ability to catch and reflect more of God than any other man.

All of these approaches are insults to the person of Jesus Christ. He was and is and can never cease to be God, and when we find Him and know Him, we are back at the ancient fountain again! Christ is all that the Godhead is!

This is the wonder, the great miracle—that by one swift, decisive, considered act of faith and prayer, our souls go back to the ancient fountain of our being, and we start over again! This means back beyond the angels, back beyond the beginning of the world, back beyond where Adam started—back to the glorious, flowing fountain we call the being of God, the triune God!

It is in Jesus Christ Himself that we find our source, our satisfaction. I think this is what John Newton perceived in the miracle of the new birth, causing him to sing, "Now rest my long-divided heart, fixed on this blissful center—rest" (from "O Happy Day" by Philip Doddridge, 1755).

Can there be any explanation for the fact that we seem to know so little of Jesus Christ even after He has made Himself and His blessings so readily available to His believing children?

Part of the answer may be found in our own human reasoning, which becomes so easily discouraged in the face of God's infinity and God's character.

Brethren, it is well for us to remember that as human beings we can never know all of the Godhead. If we were capable of knowing all of the Godhead perfectly, we would be equal to the Godhead. For illustration, we know that we cannot pour an entire quart of water into a vessel that has a capacity of less than a quart. So, you could never pour all of the Godhead into the experience of any being who is less than God Himself.

A similar kind of illustration was used long ago by ancient fathers in the church as they argued for the Trinity in the Godhead. They pointed out that God the eternal Father is an infinite God, and He is love. The very nature of love is to give itself, but the Father could not give His love fully to anyone not fully equal to Himself. Thus we have the revelation of the Son who is equal to the Father and of the eternal Father pouring out His love into the Son, who could contain it, because the Son is equal with the Father. Further, these ancient wise men reasoned, if the Father were to pour out His love on the Son, a medium of communication equal both to the Father and to the Son would be required, and this was the Holy Ghost. So we have their concept of the Trinity—the ancient Father in the fullness of His love pouring Himself through the Holy Ghost, who is in being equal to Him, into the Son who is in being equal to the Spirit and to the Father.

Certainly not all of the mystery of the Godhead can be known by man, but just as certainly, all that man can know of God in this life is revealed in Jesus Christ. When the Apostle Paul said with yearning, "That I may know Him" (Philippians 3:10), he was not speaking of intellectual knowledge, that which can be learned and memorized, but Paul was speaking of the reality of an experience, that of knowing God personally and consciously, spirit touching spirit and heart touching heart.

There are many in the churches of our day who talk some of the Christian language but who know God only by hearsay. Most of them have read some book about God. They have seen some reflection of the light of God. They may have heard some faint echo of the voice of God, but their own personal knowledge of God is very slight.

Many Christians are staking their reputations on church attendance, religious activity, social fellowship, sessions of singing—because in all of these things, they are able to lean on one another. They spend a lot of time serving as religious props for one another in Christian circles.

When Jesus was here upon the earth, the record shows that He had work to do and He also knew the necessity for activity as He preached and healed, taught and answered questions and blessed the people. He also knew the fellowship of His brethren, those who followed Him and loved Him. But these were the incidental things in Jesus' life compared to His fellowship with and personal knowledge of the Father. When Jesus went into the mountain to pray and wait on God all night, He was not alone, for He knew the conscious presence of the Father was with Him.

In our modern Christian service we are constantly pressed to do this and to do that, and to go here and go there. How often we miss completely the conscious presence of God with the result that we know God only by hearsay!

Again, part of the answer we are looking for is the fact that so many professing Christians just want to get things from God. Anyone can write a book now that will sell—just give it a title like Seventeen Ways to Get Things from God! You will have immediate sales. Or, write a book called Fourteen Ways to Have Peace of Mind—and away they go by the ton. Many people seem to be interested in knowing God for what they can get out of Him.

They do not seem to know that God wants to give Himself. He wants to impart Himself with His gifts. Any gift that He would give us would be incomplete if it were separate from the knowledge of God Himself.

If I should pray for all of the spiritual gifts listed in Paul's epistles and the Spirit of God should see fit to give me all seventeen, it would be extremely dangerous for me if, in the giving, God did not give Himself, as well.

We have mentioned creation and the fact that God has created an environment for all of His creatures. Because God made man in His image and redeemed him by the blood of the Lamb, the heart of God Himself is the true environment for the Christian. If there is grief in heaven, I think it must come from the fact that we want God's gifts, but we don't want God Himself as our environment.

I can only say that if God gives you a rose without giving Himself, He is giving you a thorn. If God gives you a garden without giving Himself, He is giving you a garden with a serpent. If He gives you wine without the knowledge of God Himself, He is giving you that with which you may destroy yourself.

I feel that we must repudiate this great, modern wave of seeking God for His benefits. The sovereign God wants to be loved for Himself and honored for Himself, but that is only part of what He wants. The other part is that He wants us to know that when we have Him, we have everything—we have all the rest. Jesus made that plain when He said, *"But seek ye first the kingdom of God, and his righteousness; and all these things shall be added unto you."* (Matthew 6:33)

It seems that Christian believers have been going through a process of indoctrination and brainwashing, so it has become easy for us to adopt a kind of creed that makes God to be our servant instead of our being God's servant.

Why should a man write and distribute a tract instructing us on "How to Pray So God Will Send You the Money You Need"? Any of us who have experienced a life and ministry of faith can tell how the Lord has met our needs. My wife and I would probably have starved in those early years of ministry if we couldn't have trusted God completely for food and everything else. Of course, we believe that God can send money to His believing children—but it becomes a pretty cheap thing to get excited about the money and fail to give the glory to Him who is the Giver!

So many are busy "using" God. Use God to get a job. Use God to give us safety. Use God to give us peace of mind. Use God to obtain success in business. Use God to provide heaven at last.

Brethren, we ought to learn—and learn it very soon—that it is much better to have God first and have God Himself even if we have only a thin dime than to have all the riches and all the influence in the world and not have God with it!

John Wesley believed that men ought to seek God alone because God is love, and he advised people in his day: "If anyone comes preaching and tells you to seek anything more than love, do not listen, do not listen!" I think in our day we are in need of such an admonition as, "Seek more of God—and seek Him for Himself alone!" If we become serious-minded about this, we would soon discover that all of the gifts of God come along with the knowledge and the presence of God Himself.

Actually, anything or anyone that keeps me from knowing God in this vital and personal way is my enemy. If it is a friend that stands in my way, the friend is an enemy. If it is a gift that stands between us, that gift is an enemy. It may be an ambition, it may be a victory in the past, it may even be a defeat which still overwhelms me—any of these allowed to stand between the Lord and myself becomes an enemy and may keep me from further knowledge of God.

Have you had any part in this cheapening of the gospel by making God your servant? Have you allowed leanness to come to your soul because you have been expecting that God would come around with a basket giving away presents?

Perhaps some of us have a tendency to think of God standing around and tossing dimes to the children as John D. Rockefeller used to do. Can it be true that Christian believers are engaged in scrambling for those shiny, new dimes and then write a tract about it, such as "I Found a Shiny Dime, and It Had the Image of God on It!"

Brethren, let's not try to compare anything like that with the deep and satisfying knowledge of God Himself. Know Him! Go on to know Him! Then, if anyone comes to quote Scriptures and argue that your experience is all wrong, you can reply, "You are a good expositor—but I happen to know my Lord, and I love Him just for Himself!"

This is all that the Lord desires for us—and it is in this that we fulfill the purpose for which He created us!

19. The un-Christlike Christian

"The average, modern Christian is not Christlike. He is quick to defend his flaws, his weaknesses and defeats in fiery, red-faced indignation!"

It seems that we have reached a time in the Christian church when it has become embarrassing to ask plainly and in so many words: "Is there anyone for spiritual perfection?"

It is apparent that many people become nervous and uncomfortable, even in our evangelical Christian circles, when we seek to bring forward this theme of spiritual perfection. I am amazed that Christians can continue to read the strong appeals of the Lord Jesus Christ and the apostles throughout the New Testament for more earnest spiritual desire—and still want to put on the brakes!

What is their concept of Christianity? Do they think it is partly religion and partly play and social fun? Do they reject a true concept of Christianity—that our spiritual life is really a battlefield, a preparation for a greater life to come? If the cross of Jesus Christ means what it should to us and we know that we must carry it and die on it and then rise and live above it, we will have a constant desire to advance and gain spiritual ground!

The nervous people who want to put on the brakes, who feel the necessity for restraint in matters of spiritual desire and yearning for perfection, often use the expression, "Let's not get fanatical about this!"

I can only ask: Is it fanaticism to want to go on until you can perfectly love God and perfectly praise Him?

Is it fanatical to find divine joy leaping up within your heart? Is it fanatical to find the willingness within your being to say, "Yes, Lord! Yes, Lord!" and thus live daily in the will of God so that you are living in heaven while you are living on earth?

If this is fanaticism, then it is the fanaticism of the Old Testament patriarchs and the Law; it is the fanaticism of the psalmist and of the prophets and the New Testament writers as well.

This would have to be the fanaticism that gave us Methodism, that gave us the Salvation Army, the fanaticism that gave birth to Moravianism and the entire Reformation. It is the fanaticism that gave us all the friends of God who held close to the truth, the fanaticism that ultimately brought our own Christian and Missionary Alliance into being.

Throughout the ages, there have been the plain saints, the simple saints, the holy people who would not surrender themselves to the common ways of the world. Unappreciated, often unknown, they were found in many places.

History tells us how they salted down the nations, even in the darkest of times. They set themselves to live by a spiritual perfection, or at least the beginning of spiritual perfection day by day. So it was that when the time of the Reformation came, there was a fertile soil into which to put the seed. Luther, even with his bull neck, could never have done what he did if there had not been a preparation by John Tawler and others like him, going up and down the land preaching this kind of spiritual desire and attainment.

You who study the Word of God know full well that a hunger for God's will is the mood and temper of the Law and of the Psalms and of the prophets and of the New Testament writers.

Those of you who have gone on to read the great books of devotion within the Christian faith know too that this yearning for perfection was the temper of all of the superior souls who have ever lived. They have written our great works of faith and love and devotion and they have composed our loftiest hymns. It is to our shame that we as unworthy spiritual descendants of those great fathers so often use their hymns without any spiritual awareness of what we are singing!

This is one of the marks of our modern time—that many are guilty of merely "nibbling" at the truth of the Christian gospel.

I wonder if you realize that, in many ways, the preaching of the Word of God is being pulled down to the level of the ignorant and spiritually obtuse. We must tell stories and jokes and entertain and amuse in order to have a few people in the audience. We do these things that we may have some reputation and that there may be money in the treasury to meet the church bills.

I believe in being honest about it—let's admit that we have to pull down the application of the gospel not to the standard of the one who is really thirsting after God, but to the one who is the most carnal, the cheapest saintling hanging on by the teeth anywhere in the kingdom of God!

In many churches Christianity has been watered down until the solution is so weak that if it were poison it would not hurt anyone, and if it were medicine it would not cure anyone!

Now I want to bring you to my postulate that most present-day Christians live sub-Christian lives.

I repeat: Most modern Christians live sub-Christian lives!

Most Christians are not joyful persons because they are not holy persons, and they are not holy persons because they are not filled with the Holy Spirit, and they are not filled with the Holy Spirit because they are not separated persons.

The Spirit cannot fill whom He cannot separate, and whom He cannot fill, He cannot make holy, and whom He cannot make holy, He cannot make happy!

There you have it—my postulate that the modern Christian, even though he has accepted Christ and has been born again, is not a joyful person because he is not a holy person.

My postulate further insists that the average modern Christian is not Christlike. The proof of this is apparent in the disposition that we find among the children of God. If I did not have some sense of prophetic vision to see down the years, and like the prophets to be willing to fall asleep not having seen the fulfillment of the promises, I would be deeply despondent to know that I have preached for years to some people who still have bad dispositional flaws. In addition, they have moral weaknesses and suffer frequent defeats. They have a dulled understanding and often live far below the standard of the Scriptures and thus outside the will of God.

The worst of it is that many in this condition will defend their flaws, their weaknesses and defeats in fiery, red-faced indignation!

We should not be too surprised by this substandard spiritual condition, for it is often described in the Bible. You will remember a warning which was spoken concerning Israel, God's people, first in the Old Testament and repeated in the New: Though the children of Israel should be as the sand by the seashore in number, only a remnant should be saved.

Our Lord Himself said in the gospel record that the love of many would wax cold. In the letters to the seven churches in the Revelation, we have descriptions of churches that function as churches but have lost their first love and are cold and have very much wrong with them spiritually.

Read in the New Testament and you will find that there were persons who refused completely the teachings of Jesus, even though He lived and served in their midst.

Stages of Christian Maturity

The point I am making here is that there are at least four different and distinct stages of Christian experience and maturity that we consistently find among the professing children of God. Lest there be misunderstanding and misinterpretation, I must make it plain that these are four very evident stages of spiritual life and disposition to be found among us every day—but not four works of grace!

I can just hear someone saying, "I have heard about two works of grace, and I have even heard of some who teach that there are three, but now Tozer is teaching four!"

No, not four works of grace!

I will refer to one of God's great souls of the past and his book, The Cloud of Unknowing. We do not know the name of the devoted saint who more than 600 years ago wrote in his pre-Elizabethan English for the purpose, as he declares it, "that God's children might go on to be 'oned' with God."

At the beginning of his book, he breathed a brief prayer of longing and devotion, and I come back to it often for the good of my own spirit.

He said, "Oh God, unto whom all hearts be open, and unto whom all will speaketh, and unto whom no privy thing is hid, I beseech Thee, so for to cleanse the intent of my heart with the unspeakable gift of Thy grace, that I may perfectly love Thee and worthily praise Thee!"

In this prayer he first acknowledges that in God's sight all hearts are open and fully known. God can see in. Even if you close your heart, lock it and throw away the key, God still sees into your heart.

"And unto whom all will speaketh"—this is one of the doctrines of the Bible and strongly emphasized in his book, that the will of a man's heart is prayer. Centuries later Montgomery expressed it: "Prayer is the soul's sincere desire unuttered or expressed." In other words, what you will in your heart is eloquent, and God is always listening to what you are willing, what you are determining to do, and what you plan.

"And unto whom no privy thing is hid"—nothing can be held as a secret from the living God.

Then, "I beseech Thee, so for to cleanse the intent of my heart with the unspeakable gift of Thy grace, that I may perfectly love Thee and worthily praise Thee."

I can discern no trace of theological fault or error in this prayer of devotion and desire breathed long ago by this saint of God.

"Oh God, fix my heart so I may perfectly love Thee and worthily praise Thee!" Nothing extreme and fanatical there. The true child of God will say "Amen" to this desire within the being to perfectly love God and worthily praise Him.

He points out, "I find four degrees and forms of Christian men's living." He names them: "common," "special," "singular" and "perfect."

He was frank in telling how Christians lived six centuries ago. I think this old saint would have been an outstanding and effective evangelist. If he had come around 600 years later, how we could have used him in our camps and conferences!

He knew the categories among Christians then, and I believe we can see them today.

There are "common" Christians, and God knows what a mob we are!

There is also the "special" Christian. He has moved on a little. Then there is the "singular" Christian, and he is unusual.

But now, this man who is our teacher for the time continues: "These first three stages, common, special and singular, may be begun and ended in this life. But the fourth, the perfect Christian may by the grace of God begin here but shall ever last on without end in the bliss of heaven."

So you see now that neither he nor I are "perfectionists" to the point that we would walk about with a benign St. Francis smile as if to say, "I am perfect; don't bother me!" We will always find that there is ground yet to be taken even though we have entered into the beginning of spiritual perfection.

Serious About Perfection

There is an interesting admonition by the author of *The Cloud of Unknowing,* in which he asks that only those who are serious about going on to perfection should read or consider his writings.

He wrote: "Now, I charge thee and I beseech thee, in the name of the Father and of the Son and of the Holy Ghost, that thou neither read this book nor write it nor speak it nor suffer it to be read, except it be such an one as hath by a true will and by a whole intent, purposed him to be a perfect follower of Christ."

He is saying, in other words, "This is such a serious and weighty matter, that no one should fool around with it, or be merely curious or casual about it—only those who have made up their minds and have a true will and a whole intent to be a perfect follower of Jesus Christ."

The old saint then says: "For my intent was never to write such things unto them, therefore, I would that they meddle not herewith, neither they nor any of these curious persons, either lettered or unlettered."

So, if the only interest you have in the deeper spiritual life is based on curiosity, it is not enough, regardless of your education or scholarship!

In our day we have seen a great revival of interest in mysticism, supposedly a great interest in the deeper life. But I find that much of this interest is academic and based on curiosity. We become interested in aspects of the deeper Christian life much as we become interested in mastering the yo-yo or folk songs or dabbling in Korean architecture or anything else that intrigues us. You can go anywhere now and buy a book about the deeper life because there are curious persons who are swelling the market.

But this saint of old said, "I never want any curious, merely curious person to even bother about this, for he will never get anything out of it."

I think I hear him saying to me as well, "Tozer, by the grace of God in the power of the Trinity, I beseech you do not preach this unless people are determined in their hearts to be perfect followers of Christ."

But it is Jesus' blood that makes the difference, and because of this hope that by the blood of Jesus we may be worthy to listen, I differ with the old saint in this point.

Brethren, I am not willing to withhold the open secrets of spiritual power from those who can receive them just because there are others who cannot. I am not going to withhold the open secret of the victorious life from those who can understand it and desire it because of those who are merely curious and without desire. We must leave the sorting out to God. The testing in the matters of spiritual life is by the Spirit of God, not by pastors and preachers.

We have many examples of men and women being tested unconsciously in the Scriptures, for the Holy Spirit rarely tells a person that he is about to be tested.

When you go to a doctor for an examination or take a scheduled examination in the classroom, the testing is conscious and purposeful. Consciously and knowingly, you are taking a test to find out where you stand or whether you can fulfill the requirements.

But in the Scriptures the testing times were very rarely known to those being tested, and that is a sobering thought.

Abraham was being tested when he was asked to leave Ur of the Chaldees, but he did not know it. And when the Lord asked Abraham to take his only son up into the mountain, he thought he was being ordered. He did not know that he was being tested.

Peter was unconsciously tested. Paul was tested. There comes a time when we have heard enough truth and had sufficient opportunity and the Holy Spirit says, "Today this man is going to have his test!"

The people of Israel in their time of testing came to Kadesh-barnea and instead of crossing into the land, they said, "We will not go over." They were unconscious of the testing, and they went back. They did not realize that they were sentencing themselves to forty years of

aimless, useless wandering in the desert sands. The Lord had not said
to them, "Now stand up, everyone. Breathe deeply! This is going to
be a test!" He simply let them make their own test, and they flunked
it.

It is a solemn and frightening thing in this world of sin and flesh and
devils, to realize that about eighty or ninety percent of the people
whom God is testing will flunk the test!

The Lord will do His own sorting out, and all of us should be aware
that we are in a time when every day is a day of testing. Some come
to their Kadesh-barnea and turn back. Some simply stand and look
across the river. They are only curious.

Is there anyone for spiritual perfection—anyone with an honest desire to be Christlike—to be more like Jesus Christ every day?

20.False Teaching

Beloved, when I gave all diligence to write unto you of the common salvation,

it was needful for me to write unto you,

and exhort you that ye should earnestly contend for the faith

which was once delivered unto the saints.

For there are certain men crept in unawares,

who were before of old ordained to this condemnation,

ungodly men, turning the grace of our God into lasciviousness,

and denying the only Lord God, and our Lord Jesus Christ.

JUDE 3-4

Peter, along with the other apostles, understood that the church faced an increasing array of false teaching and heresy. They knew by the whisper of the Holy Ghost within them that it was important to lay down a strong defense against false teaching, and that the Christian needed to stand firm against everything that was not in harmony with the Scriptures. They needed to prepare the individual Christian to recognize false teaching and make a stand against it.

Much of the New Testament is given over to instructions in this regard. The apostle Paul spent a large amount of time writing along this line. Many of his epistles were written to combat some false teaching that had arisen in the church he had started.

An apostle that we do not hear very much about is Jude, a brother of Christ. He planned to write an encouraging letter, just as you might sit down to write your friends a letter of encouragement. He planned to write about what he called our "common salvation." But he was moved and impressed by the Holy Ghost to write something else altogether. An unpleasant circumstance had arisen, forcing him to write quite another kind of letter from the good encouraging letter he had planned. Certain men had crept into the fellowship unnoticed. Those men were men of evil personal lives and had been foreseen and condemned by the Lord Himself when He was with the disciples. They taught doctrine contrary to Christian faith. Jude writes to arouse the victims of these teachers to contend for the truth.

What do we mean by false teaching? It signifies teaching that things are otherwise than what they are. Both physical things and spiritual things are what they are. You can put a period after that. And when we have discovered or had revealed to us the facts about them, either things material or things spiritual, then we are morally required to acknowledge those facts and make our teachings conform to them. That is all so very simple that I almost apologize for saying it, but it is the broad framework upon which everything else must hang—that things are as they are. Whether we like them or not, that is the way they are. God made things, and things are. Physical and material things are and spiritual things are. It is our business to find out how they are, to accept them as they are and then make our teaching conform to them as they are.

Correct doctrine is of vital importance because it is simply the teaching of things as they are. Telling the truth about things is finding out what they are and then conforming my statement to their facts.

This is also so with spiritual truths. When a truth has been revealed in the Bible, our business is to find out what that truth is and then in all of our teaching conform to that truth—not edit it or change it, but let it stand just as it is. It is the truth of God declared as it is, and do not try to change it.

It would be ridiculous of me to try by some twist of logic or sophistry to make this be August when it's July, or to make it be the ninth when it's the third, or to make this be winter when it's summer, or to make this country to be Canada when it is the United States. Truth is just as it is. God Almighty made the world to be a mathematical universe and all things run according to mathematical laws. He has a moral world, which runs according to moral laws that are as exact and unchanging as His mathematical laws.

Nonconformity to the truth anywhere brings disaster. Let an engineer be wrong about a position, let him build according to that wrong concept and his building will collapse around him. Let a navigator be wrong about his calculations and he will run on a rock and his old ship will shudder as it runs onto a sandbar or a rock and will settle in the water and sink out of sight. The navigator has not gone according to truth.

Nonconformity always brings disaster wherever it may be. And the vastness and hugeness of the disaster depend upon the high level or low level of the facts we have before us. False teaching is the falsifying of data about God, ourselves, sin and Christ.

The Nature of False Teaching

First, any false teaching must begin with the wrong concept of God. Nobody holding the right concept of God can go far wrong in anything else. And all the basic great mistakes that have been made, the great fundamental errors, have all rested down around concepts of God. Men are not willing to let God be what He says He is. They are always trying to change God and trying to make Him to be other than what He is.

God is, and we had better accept Him as He is. God is, and the angels want Him to be what He is. God is, and the elders, saints and heavenly creatures want Him to be what He is. We better want Him to be what He is and conform to what He is. Any structure or foundation that is crooked will bring the structure down in time. It will either sink or collapse or lean or fall over, but it will not stand long. Or if it does, it will lean as the leaning tower of Pisa in Italy.

Of all the foundations, God is the most important, because God is God and He made the heaven and earth and all the things therein. It would be a great error on the part of a man or woman to go a lifetime thinking they were talking to the God of heaven and earth and find they were talking to a god they had confounded out of their own imaginations.

For me to pray a lifetime and preach a lifetime about God in a way that was not true to what God is really would be a terrible, tragic calamity. To believe in a God that was a composite of ideas drawn from philosophy and psychology and other religions and superstitions would be eternally disastrous. No, God is what He is. And we had better learn what God is and then conform our teachings to God.

Think of the attributes of God. They all comprise the nature of one God. If we eliminate or ignore any of those attributes, we come away with something that is less than God. For example, if you take all the justice, judgment and hatred of sin out of the nature of God, you have nothing left but a soft God. And those who have taken love and grace out end up with nothing but a God of judgment. Take away the personality of God and you have nothing but a mathematical God like the God of the scientists. All these are false, inadequate conceptions of God.

Our God is a God of justice and a God of grace; and while He is the God of righteousness, He also is the God of mercy. And while He is a God of mathematical exactness, He is also a God that could take babies in His arms and pat their heads and smile. He is a God that can forgive and a God that does forgive. So we had better make the study of this Bible the business of our lives to find out what God is and then conform our views to God.

The second thing where we make a mistake is that any wrong idea of God is bound to give us a wrong idea of ourselves. Some people approach God through science and the study of anthropology; but anthropology without theology is bound to arrive at an error. You and I can only explain ourselves in the light of the doctrine that God made us out of the dust of the ground and blew into our nostrils the breath of life, and so man became a living soul. Science has discovered many things about God, but they have not discovered it in context. They have not begun with God and reason down to His world; they have begun with the world and tried to reason up to God and stop short of finding God. The result is tragic for everybody.

If man is wrong about God, then he is bound to be wrong about himself. If he is wrong about the artist, then he will be wrong about the picture. If he is wrong about the potter, then he will be wrong about the vessel. If he is wrong about God, then he will be wrong about the creature. While multiplying scientific facts all around us, which are wrong because they have left God out, they say there is no God. Or if there is a God, He is a God of mathematics and laws but not the God the Bible makes Him out to be. That is all wrong, and you cannot know the truth about yourself unless you first know the truth about God. You came from the hand of God, and back to God you must go for better, for worse, for judgment or for blessings.

So when we take God in, understand God and let God be what He claims to be, and believe about ourselves what God says about us, we are believing rightly. If you believe you are any better than God says you are, you are in error. If you believe you are any different from what God says you are, you are in error. You will falsify the data. Somebody has falsified the data and made you a victim. Believe about yourself what God says about you. Believe you are as bad as

God says you are, and believe you are as far from Him as God says you are, and then believe in Christ who can come as near to Him as He says you can, and accept what He says about you as being truth.

Then there is sin. Sin cannot be understood until we believe in God and believe what God has said about ourselves. Sin is that intrusive phenomenon, that ever-present, ubiquitous phenomenon. There it is—hatred, lies, dishonesty, murder, crime, dishonesty, justice, law, police, jails, locks and graves. But there are those who would deny it and, of course, that is falsifying the data. There are those who would rename sin, and they are falsifying the data. There are those who would treat it as a disease, and they are falsifying data.

God said that sin is a breaking of the law. God said it is rebellion against His will. God says that it is a nature inherited from our fathers and mothers. God says that it is an act against the faith and love and mercy of God. God says it is rebellion against constituted authority of the Majesty on High. God says it is iniquity and personally chargeable to the one who commits it. And God says, "The soul that sinneth, it shall die" (Ezek. 18:20). We had better believe about sin what God says about sin or we will be falsifying the data. Falsified data in spiritual things is more terribly wrong and will bring more terrible consequences then falsifying data in material things.

The doctor who miscounts the amount of a medicine that he gives a patient may kill the patient, which would be only to destroy a body. The preacher who misjudges or miscounts the truth concerning sin and man and God will damn his hearer, which is infinitely more terrible. Truth concerning God means I must accept God's sovereignty, God's holiness, God's justice, God's grace, God's love and all the Bible says about God. Concerning me, it requires that I must believe myself a fallen image of God, one who wants more of His image but fell short.

Fourth is Christ Himself. If I do not have the right concept of God and of myself and of sin, then I will have a twisted and imperfect concept of Christ. I have no hesitation in saying that it is my honest and charitable conviction that the Christ of the average religion today is not the Christ of the Bible at all. He is a manufactured Christ, the Christ painted on canvas, the Christ drawn from cheap poetry, a Christ of the liberal and the soft and timid person. He is an imitation Christ that has not in Him the iron and the fury and the anger, as well as the love and grace and mercy. If I have a wrong conception of myself, I have a dangerous conception of sin. And if I have a dangerous conception of sin, I have a degraded conception of Christ.

So here is the way it works. God is reduced and man is degraded and sin is underestimated and Christ is disparaged. No wonder the Jews said the terrible things they said. I recommend reading the book of Jude once. Get your teeth filed to a sharp eating edge, and then get your teeth into something substantial. Dare to believe something and dare to stand for God. In this awful day of so-called tolerance, people are ready to believe anything.

But ye, beloved, building up yourselves on your most holy faith, praying in the Holy Ghost, keep yourselves in the love of God, looking for the mercy of our Lord Jesus Christ unto eternal life. And of some have compassion, making a difference: And others save with fear, pulling them out of the fire; hating even the garment spotted by the flesh (Jude 20-23).

We are not called to smile and smile and smile. We are called sometimes to frown and rebuke with all long-suffering and doctrine. We must contend but not be contentious. We must preserve truth but injure no man. We must destroy error but not harm people. Some men were wrong in earlier days; they contended and, in contending, they became contentious. Trying to preserve truth, they destroyed those who held error. This is wrong. Let us preserve truth but injure no man.

Countering False Teaching

As Frederick W. Faber (1814-1863) writes in his hymn "Faith of Our Fathers":

Faith of our fathers, we will love

Both friend and foe in all our strife;

And preach Thee, too, as love knows how

By kindly words and virtuous life.

"Building up yourselves on your most holy faith." Are you these days building up yourselves? Have you read a book of the Bible through recently? Have you done any memorization of the Scriptures? Have you sought to know God? Are you looking to the radio and TV for your religion, or have you a Bible, and do you study it?

"Praying in the Holy Ghost." I do not hesitate to say that most praying is not in the Holy Ghost. The reason we do not pray in the Holy Ghost is because we do not have the Holy Ghost in us. No man can pray in the Spirit except his heart is a habitation to the Spirit. It is only as the Holy Ghost has unlimited sway within us that we are able to pray in the Holy Ghost. I do not hesitate to say that five minutes of prayer in the Holy Ghost will be worth more than one year of mis-praying that is not in the Holy Ghost.

"Keep yourselves in the love of God." Be true to the faith but be charitable to those who are in error. Never feel any contempt for anybody. No Christian has any right to feel contempt, for contempt is an emotion. It can only come out of pride, which is an open door for the enemy. So let us be an open tent; let us be charitable and loving through it all while we keep ourselves in the love of God. And, if we love God, we will also love God's.

"Looking for the mercy of our Lord Jesus Christ unto eternal life." And of course, that is the second coming of Jesus, looking for Jesus Christ's coming. It is wonderful to me that His mercy will show itself at His coming. Even His mercy will show itself then as it did on the cross, as it does when receiving sinners, as it does in patiently looking after us Christians; and it will show itself at the coming of Jesus Christ unto eternal life.

"Some have compassion, making a difference; And others save with fear, pulling them out of the fire; hating even the garment spotted by the flesh." There is a charge that we should win others, that we should do everything in our power to bring others to Christ, saving them with fear, pulling them out of the fire. John Wesley, all his life, referred to himself as the brand plucked from the burning. He knew he was on fire, already he was in the hot flames of hell when Jesus Christ grabbed him out of the fiery pit, extinguished the fire by His own blood and Wesley became the Wesley we know. He never dared to rise and think of himself as a great Oxford man or a great genius, but always thought of himself as a brand plucked from the burning. And now we look forward to Jesus Christ's coming, looking for the mercy of our Jesus Christ. Here was what the old silk weaver Gerhard Tersteegen (1697–1769) said about Christ:

There is a balm for every pain,

A medicine for all sorrow;

The eye turned backward to the Cross,

And forward to the morrow.

Some of the old saints in days gone by called the Communion service, medicine of immortality. You could not follow them in every one of their beliefs, but in that I think they were right. Medicine for all sorrow, an eye turned backward to the cross and forward to the morrow. The morrow of the glory and the song when He shall come. The morrow of the harping and the balm and the welcome home.

Meantime, in His beloved hand are ways.

Meantime, what are we going to do? Give up to the heat?

Meantime, what are we going to do? Give up to the liberals?

Meantime, what are we going to do? Give up to the dead church?

Meantime, what are we going to do? Give up to those who have chosen to walk in the low shadow of Christianity?

Never!

Dare to contend without being contentious. Dare to preserve truth without hurting people. Dare to love and be charitable and, meantime, there is rest and comfort for the weary one who lays his head upon His breast.

Let us by the grace of God, with charity for all and hatred for none, but determination to be loyal to truth if it kills us, put our chin a little higher and our knees a little lower, and let's look a little further into the throne of God, for Jesus Christ sits at the right hand of God the Father Almighty. And let us be courageous, attentive, severe but kind. Let us pray in the Holy Ghost, keep ourselves in the love of God, build ourselves up in the most holy faith and win all we can until the day of the glory and the song.

Amen.

21. Temperament's Role in Religious Views

A celebrated American preacher once advanced the novel theory that the various denominations with their different doctrinal emphases served a useful purpose as gathering places for persons of similar temperaments. Christians, he suggested, tend to gravitate toward others of like mental types. Hence the denominations.

This is undoubtedly oversimplification carried to the point of error. There are too many persons of dissimilar temperaments in every denomination to support such a sweeping classification. Yet I believe that we have here an instance where an error may serve to point up a truth, the truth being that temperament has a great deal to do with our religious views and with the emphases we lay on spiritual matters generally.

It may be a bit difficult to determine which is cause and which effect, but I have noticed that historically Calvinism has flourished among peoples of a markedly phlegmatic disposition. While it is true that Jacob Arminius was a Dutchman, on the whole the Dutch people appear temperamentally quite suited to Calvinism. On the other hand, it would be hard to imagine a Calvinistic Spaniard or Italian. Isolated instances there certainly are, but for the most part the buoyant, volatile, mandolin playing Latin does not take naturally to long periods of meditation on the divine sovereignty and the eternal decrees.

While we all pride ourselves that we draw our beliefs from the Holy Scriptures, along those border lines where good men disagree, we may unconsciously take sides with our temperament. Cast of mind may easily determine our views when the Scriptures are not clear.

People may be classified roughly into two psychological types, the gay and the sombre, and it is easy to see how each type will be attracted to the doctrinal views that agree most naturally with its own mental cast. The Calvinist, for instance, never permits himself to become too happy, while the Arminian tends to equate gravity of disposition with coldness of heart and tries to cure it with a revival.

No Calvinist could have written the radiant hymns of Bernard of

Clairvaux or Charles Wesley. Calvinism never produced a Christian mystic, unless we except John Newton who was near to being a mystic and did write a few hymns almost as radiant as those of Bernard.

To square the records, however, it should be said that if the Calvinist does not rise as high, he usually stays up longer. He places more emphasis on the Holy Scriptures which never change, while his opposite number (as the newspapers say) tends to judge his spiritual condition by the state of his feelings, which change constantly. This may be the reason that so many Calvinistic churches remain orthodox for centuries, at least in doctrine, while many churches of the Arminian persuasion often go liberal in one generation.

I realise that I am doing a bit of oversimplifying on my own here; still I believe there is more than a germ of truth in the whole thing. Anyway, I am less concerned with the effect of temperament on the historic church, which obviously I can do nothing about, than with its effect upon my own soul and the souls of my readers, whom I may be able to influence somewhat.

Whether or not my broader conclusions are sound, there would seem to be no reason to doubt that we naturally tend to interpret Scripture in the light (or shadow) of our own temperament and let our peculiar mental cast decide the degree of importance we attach to various religious doctrines and practices.

The odd thing about this human quirk is that it prospers most where there is the greatest amount of religious freedom. The authoritarian churches that tell their adherents exactly what to believe and where to lay their emphasis produce a fair degree of uniformity among their members. By stretching everyone on the bed of Procrustes they manage to lengthen or trim back the individual temperament to their liking.

The free Protestant, who is still permitted a certain amount of private interpretation, is much more likely to fall into the trap of temperament. Exposure to this temptation is one price he pays for his freedom.

The minister above all others should look deep into his own heart to discover the reason for his more pronounced views. It is not enough to draw himself up and declare with dignity that he preaches the Bible and nothing but the Bible. That claim is made by every man who stands in sincerity to declare the truth; but truth has many facets and the man of God is in grave danger of revealing only a limited few to his people, and those the ones he by disposition favors most.

One cannot imagine Francis of Assisi preaching Edward's sermon, "Sinners in the Hands of an Angry God," nor can we picture Jonathan Edwards preaching to the birds or calling upon sun and moon and wind and stars to join him in praising the Lord. Yet both were good men who loved God deeply and trusted Christ completely. Many other factors besides temperament must not be overlooked.

Are we then to accept the bias of disposition as something inevitable? Are we to allow our religious views to be dictated by ancestors long dead whose genes still stir within us? By no means. The Scriptures, critical self-discipline, honesty of heart and increased trust in the inward operations of the Holy Spirit will save us from being too greatly influenced by temperament.

22.Boredom with Christianity

That there is something gravely wrong with evangelical Christianity today is not likely to be denied by any serious-minded person acquainted with the facts. Just what is wrong is not so easy to determine.

In examining the situation myself, I find nature and reason in conflict within me, for I tend by temperament to want to settle everything with a sweep of the pen. But reason advises caution; nothing is that simple, and we must be careful to distinguish cause from effect. As every doctor knows there is a wide difference between the disease and the symptoms; and every Christian knows that there is a big difference between cause and effect in the sphere of religion.

At the root of our spiritual trouble lie a number of causes and these causes have effects, but which is cause and which effect is not always known. I suspect that many things currently under attack by our evangelists and pastors (and editors, for that matter) are not the causes of our troubles but the effects of causes that lie deeper. We treat the symptoms and wonder why the patient does not get well. Or, to change the figure, we lay down a heavy fire against nothing more substantial than the cloud of dust raised by marching enemy troops long gone by.

One mark of the low state of affairs among us is religious boredom. Whether this is a thing in itself or merely a symptom of the thing, I do not know for sure, though I suspect that it is the latter. And that it is found to some degree almost everywhere among Christians is too evident to be denied.

Boredom is, of course, a state of mind resulting from trying to maintain an interest in something that holds no trace of interest for us (the boss's jokes, say, or that lecture on the care and nurture of dahlias to which we went because we could not resist the enthusiastic urging of a friend). No one is bored by what he can in good conscience walk away from. Boredom comes when a man must try to hear with relish what for want of relish he hardly hears at all.

By this definition there is certainly much boredom in religion these days. The businessman on a Sunday morning whose mind is on golf can scarcely disguise his lack of interest in the sermon he is compelled to hear. The housewife who is unacquainted with the learned theological or philosophical jargon of the speaker; the young couple who feel a tingle of love for each other but who neither love nor know the One about whom the choir is singing—these cannot escape the low-grade mental pain we call boredom while they struggle to keep their attention focused upon the service.

All these are too courteous to admit to others that they are bored and possibly too timid to admit it even to themselves, but I believe that a bit of candid confession would do us all good.

When Moses tarried in the mount, Israel became bored with the faith that sees the invisible and clamored for a god they could see and touch. And they displayed a great deal more enthusiasm for the golden calf than they did over the Lord God of Abraham.

Later they tired of manna and complained against the monotony of their diet. On their petulant insistence they finally got flesh to eat, and that to their own undoing.

Those Christians who belong to the evangelical wing of the church (which I firmly believe is the only one that even approximates New Testament Christianity) have over the last half-century shown an increasing impatience with things invisible and eternal and have demanded and got a host of things visible and temporal to satisfy their fleshly appetites. Without Biblical authority, or any other right under the sun, carnal religious leaders have introduced a host of attractions that serve no purpose except to provide entertainment for the retarded saints.

It is now common practice in most evangelical churches to offer the people, especially the young people, a maximum of entertainment and a minimum of serious instruction.

It is scarcely possible in most places to get anyone to attend a meeting where the only attraction is God. One can only conclude that God's professed children are bored with Him, for they must be wooed to meeting with a stick of striped candy in the form of religious movies, games and refreshments.

This has influenced the whole pattern of church life, and even brought into being a new type of church architecture, designed to house the golden calf.

So we have the strange anomaly of orthodoxy in creed and heterodoxy in practice. The striped-candy technique has been so fully integrated into our present religious thinking that it is simply taken for granted. Its victims never dream that it is not a part of the teachings of Christ and His apostles.

Any objection to the carryings on of our present golden-calf Christianity is met with the triumphant reply, "But we are winning them!" And winning them to what? To true discipleship? To cross-carrying? To self-denial? To separation from the world? To crucifixion of the flesh? To holy living? To nobility of character? To a despising of the world's treasures? To hard self-discipline? To love for God? To total committal to Christ? Of course the answer to all these questions is no.

We are paying a frightful price for our religious boredom. And that at the moment of the world's mortal peril.

23.Sentimentalizing Christianity

It is vital to any understanding of ourselves and our fellowmen that we believe what is written in the Scriptures about human society, that it is fallen, alienated from God and in rebellion against His laws.

In these days of togetherness, even the true Christian is hard put to it to believe what God has spoken about men and their relation to each other and to God; for what He has spoken is never complimentary to men.

There is plenty of good news in the Bible, but there is never any flattery or back scratching. Seen one way, the Bible is a book of doom. It condemns all men as sinners and declares that the soul that sinneth shall die. Always it pronounces sentence against society before it offers mercy; and if we will not own the validity of the sentence, we cannot admit the need for mercy.

The coming of Jesus Christ to the world has been so sentimentalized that it means now something utterly alien to the Biblical teaching concerning it. Soft human pity has been substituted for God's mercy in the minds of millions, a pity that has long ago degenerated into self-pity. The blame for man's condition has been shifted to God, and Christ's dying for the world has been twisted into an act of penance on God's part. In the drama of redemption man is viewed as Miss Cinderella who has long been oppressed and mistreated, but now through the heroic deeds of earth's noblest Son is about to don her radiant apparel and step forth a queen.

This is humanism romantically tinted with Christianity, a humanism that takes sides with rebels and excuses those who by word, thought and deed would glorify fallen men and if possible overthrow the glorious high Throne in the heavens.

According to this philosophy men are never really to blame for anything, the exception being the man who insists that men are indeed to blame for something. In this dim world of pious sentiment all religions are equal and any man who insists that salvation is by Jesus Christ alone is a bigot and a boor.

So we pool our religious light, which if the truth is told is little more than darkness visible; we discuss religion on television and in the press as a kind of game, much as we discuss art and philosophy, accepting as one of the ground rules of the game that there is no final test of truth and that the best religion is a composite of the best in all religions. So we have truth by majority vote, and thus saith the Lord by common consent.

One characteristic of this sort of thing is its timidity. That religion may be very precious to some persons is admitted, but never important enough to cause division or risk hurting anyone's feelings. In all our discussions there must never be any trace of intolerance; but we obviously forget that the most fervent devotees of tolerance are invariably intolerant of everyone who speaks about God with certainty. And there must be no bigotry, which is the name given to spiritual assurance by those who do not enjoy it.

The desire to please may be commendable enough under certain circumstances, but when pleasing men means displeasing God, it is an unqualified evil and should have no place in the Christian's heart. To be right with God has often meant to be in trouble with men. This is such a common truth that one hesitates to mention it, yet it appears to have been overlooked by the majority of Christians today.

There is a notion abroad that to win a man we must agree with him. Actually, the exact opposite is true. G. K. Chesterton remarked that each generation has had to be converted by the man who contradicted it most. The man who is going in a wrong direction will never be set right by the affable religionist who falls into step beside him and goes the same way. Someone must place himself across the path and insist that the straying man turn around and go in the right direction.

There is of course a sense in which we are all in this terrible human mess together, and for this reason there are certain areas of normal activity where we can all agree. The Christian will not disagree merely to be different, but wherever the moral standards and religious views of society differ from the teachings of Christ he will disagree flatly. He will not admit the validity of human opinion when the Word of God is clear.

Some things are not debatable; there is no other side to them. There is only God's side.

When men believe God, they speak boldly. When they doubt, they confer. Much current religious talk is but uncertainty rationalizing itself; and this they call "engaging in the contemporary dialogue." It is impossible to imagine Moses or Elijah so occupied.

All great Christian leaders have been dogmatic. To such men two plus two made four.

Anyone who insisted upon denying it or suspending judgment upon it was summarily dismissed as frivolous. They were only interested in a meeting of minds if the minds agreed to meet on holy ground. We could use some gentle dogmatists these days.

24.Negotiating the Non-Negotiable

Will Rogers once opined that a sure way to prevent war would be to abolish peace conferences.

Of course, Will, as usual, had his tongue in his cheek; he meant only to poke fun at the weak habit of substituting talk for action. Still, there is more than a little uncomfortable truth in his remark.

This above all others is the age of much talk. Hardly a day passes that the newspapers do not carry one or another of the headlines "Talks to Begin" or "Talks to Continue" or "Talks to Resume." The idea behind this endless official chatter is that all differences between men result from their failure to understand each other; if each can discover exactly what the other thinks, they will find to their delight that they are really in full agreement after all. Then they have only to smile, shake hands, go home and live happily ever after.

At the bottom of all this is the glutenous, one-world, all-men-are-brothers philosophy that has taken such hold on the minds of many of our educators and politicians. (The hard-headed realists of the Communist camp know better; maybe that is why they are making such alarming advances throughout the world while the all-men-are-brothers devotees are running around in confusion, trying to keep smiling if it kills them.)

Tolerance, charity, understanding, good will, patience and other such words and ideas are lifted from the Bible, misunderstood and applied indiscriminately to every situation. The kidnapper will not steal your baby if you only try to understand him; the burglar caught sneaking into your house with a gun is not really bad, he is just hungry for fellowship and togetherness; the gang killer taking his victim for a one-way ride can be dissuaded from committing murder if someone will only have faith in his basic goodness and have a talk with him.

And this is supposed to be the teaching of Jesus, which it most certainly is not.

The big thing now is to "keep in touch." Never let the dialogue die and never accept any decision as final; everything can be negotiated.

Where there is life there is talk and where there is talk there is hope. "As long as they are talking, they are not shooting at each other," say the advocates of the long palaver, and in so saying they forget Pearl Harbour.

This yen to confer has hit the church also, which is not strange since almost everything the church is doing these days has been suggested to her by the world. I observe with pained amusement how many water boys of the pulpit in their effort to be prophets are standing up straight and tall and speaking out boldly in favor of ideas that have been previously fed into their minds by the psychiatrists, the sociologists, the novelists, the scientists and the secular educators. The ability to appraise correctly the direction public opinion is moving is a gift not to be despised; by means of it, we preachers can talk loudly and still stay out of trouble.

A new Decalogue has been adopted by the neo-Christians of our day, the first word of which reads, "Thou shalt not disagree"; and a new set of Beatitudes too, which begins "Blessed are they that tolerate everything, for they shall not be made accountable for anything." It is now the accepted thing to talk over religious differences in public with the understanding that no one will try to convert another or point out errors in his belief. The purpose of these talks is not to confront truth, but to discover how the followers of other religions think and thus benefit from their views as we hope they will from ours.

It is a truism that people agree to disagree only about matters they consider unimportant. No man is tolerant when it concerns his life or the life of his child, and no one will agree to negotiate over any religious matter he considers vital to his eternal welfare.

Imagine Moses agreeing to take part in a panel discussion with Israel over the golden calf; or Elijah engaging in a gentlemanly dialogue with the prophets of Baal. Or try to picture our Lord Jesus Christ seeking a meeting of minds with the Pharisees to iron out differences; or Athanasius trying to rise above his differences with Arius in order to achieve union on a higher level; or Luther crawling into the presence of the pope in the name of a broader Christian fellowship.

The desire to be liked even if not respected is a great weakness in any man's character, and in that of a minister of Jesus Christ it is a weakness wholly inexcusable. The popular image of the man of God as a smiling, congenial, asexual religious mascot whose handshake is always soft and whose head is always bobbing in the perpetual Yes of universal acquiescence is not the image found in the Scriptures of truth.

The blessing of God is promised to the peacemaker, but the religious negotiator had better watch his step. The ability to settle quarrels between members of God's household is a heavenly gift and one that should be assiduously cultivated. The discerning soul who can reconcile separated friends by prayer and appeal to the Scriptures is worth his weight in diamonds.

That is one thing, but the effort to achieve unity at the expense of truth and righteousness is another. To seek to be friends with those who will not be the friends of Christ is to be a traitor to our Lord. Darkness and light can never be brought together by talk. Some things are not negotiable.

25.Does God Always Answer Prayer?

Contrary to popular opinion, the cultivation of a psychology of uncritical belief is not an unqualified good, and if carried too far it may be a positive evil. The whole world has been booby-trapped by the devil, and the deadliest trap of all is the religious one.

Error never looks so innocent as when it is found in the sanctuary.

One field where harmless-looking but deadly traps appear in great profusion is the field of prayer. There are more sweet notions about prayer than could be contained in a large book, all of them wrong and all highly injurious to the souls of men.

I think of one such false notion that is found often in pleasant places consorting smilingly with other notions of unquestionable orthodoxy. It is that God always answers prayer.

This error appears among the saints as a kind of all-purpose philosophic therapy to prevent any disappointed Christian from suffering too great a shock when it becomes evident to him that his prayer expectations are not being fulfilled. It is explained that God always answers prayer, either by saying Yes or by saying No, or by substituting something else for the desired favor.

Now, it would be hard to invent a neater trick than this to save face for the petitioner whose requests have been rejected for non-obedience. Thus when a prayer is not answered he has but to smile brightly and explain, "God said No." It is all so very comfortable. His wobbly faith is saved from confusion and his conscience is permitted to lie undisturbed. But I wonder if it is honest.

To receive an answer to prayer as the Bible uses the term and as Christians have understood it historically, two elements must be present: (1) A clear-cut request made to God for a specific favour. (2) A clear-cut granting of that favour by God in answer to the request. There must be no semantic twisting, no changing of labels, no altering of the map during the journey to help the embarrassed tourist to find himself.

When we go to God with a request that He modify the existing situation for us, that is, that He answer prayer, there are two conditions that we must meet: (1) We must pray in the will of God and (2) we must be on what old-fashioned Christians often call "praying ground"; that is, we must be living lives pleasing to God.

It is futile to beg God to act contrary to His revealed purposes. To pray with confidence the petitioner must be certain that his request falls within the broad will of God for His people.

The second condition is also vitally important. God has not placed Himself under obligation to honour the requests of worldly, carnal or disobedient Christians. He hears and answers the prayers only of those who walk in His way. *"Beloved, if our heart condemn us not, then have we confidence toward God. And whatsoever we ask, we receive of him, because we keep his commandments, and do those things that are pleasing in his sight ... If ye abide in me, and my words abide in you, ye shall ask what ye will, and it shall be done unto you."* (1 John 3:21-22; John 15:7)

God wants us to pray and He wants to answer our prayers, but He makes our use of prayer as a privilege to commingle with His use of prayer as a discipline. To receive answers to prayer we must meet God's terms. If we neglect His commandments, our petitions will not be honoured. He will alter situations only at the request of obedient and humble souls.

The God-always-answers-prayer sophistry leaves the praying man without discipline. By the exercise of this bit of smooth casuistry he ignores the necessity to live soberly, righteously and godly in this present world. He actually takes God's flat refusal to answer his prayer as the very answer itself.

Of course such a man will not grow in holiness; he will never learn how to wrestle and wait; he will never know correction; he will not hear the voice of God calling him forward; he will never arrive at the place where he is morally and spiritually fit to have his prayers answered. His wrong philosophy has ruined him.

That is why I turn aside to expose the bit of bad theology upon which his bad philosophy is founded. The man who accepts it never knows where he stands; he never knows whether or not he has true faith, for if his request is not granted, he avoids the implication by the simple dodge of declaring that God switched the whole thing around and gave him something else. He will not allow himself to shoot at a target, so he cannot tell how good or how bad a marksman he is.

Of certain persons James says plainly: "Ye ask, and receive not, because ye ask amiss, that ye may consume it upon your lusts." From that brief sentence we may learn that God refuses some requests because they who make them are not morally worthy to receive the answer. But this means nothing to the one who has been seduced into the belief that God always answers prayer. When such a man asks and receives not, he passes his hand over the hat and comes up with the answer in some other form. One thing he clings to with great tenacity: God never turns anyone away, but invariably grants every request.

The truth is that God always answers the prayer that accords with His will as revealed in the Scriptures, provided the one who prays is obedient and trustful. Further than this we dare not go.

If unanswered prayer continues in a congregation over an extended period of time, the chill of discouragement will settle over the praying people. If we continue to ask and ask and ask, like petulant children, never expecting to get what we ask for but continuing to whine for it, we will become chilled within our beings.

If we continue in our prayers and never get answers, the lack of results will tend to confirm the natural unbelief of our hearts. Remember this: the human heart by nature is filled with unbelief. Unbelief, not disobedience, was the first sin. While disobedience was the first recorded sin, behind the act of disobedience was the sin of unbelief, else the act of disobedience would not have taken place.

The fact of unanswered prayer will also encourage the idea that religion is unreal, and this idea is held by many people in our day. "Religion is completely subjective," they tell us. "There is nothing real about it."

It is true that there may be nothing tangible to which religion can be referred. If I use the word lake, everyone thinks of a large body of water. When I use the word star, everyone thinks of a heavenly body. But when I use such words as faith and belief and God and heaven, there is not any image of a reality which is known to people and to which their minds immediately refer. To most people, those are just words—like pixies and goblins. So there is a false idea of unreality in our hearts when we pray and pray and pray, and receive no answers.

Perhaps worst of all is the fact that our failures in prayer leave the enemy in possession of the field. The worst part about the failure of a military drive is not the loss of men or the loss of face but the fact that the enemy is left in possession of the field. In the spiritual sense, this is both a tragedy and a disaster. The devil ought to be on the run, always fighting a rear guard action. Instead, this blasphemous enemy smugly and scornfully holds his position, and the people of God let him have it. No wonder the work of the Lord is greatly retarded. Little wonder the work of God stands still!

26.Stopped Dead in Your Tracks?

I blame faulty exposition of the New Testament for stopping many Christians dead in their tracks, causing them to shrug off any suggestion that there is still spiritual advance and progress beckoning them on.

The position of some would-be teachers is that when you come into the kingdom of God by faith, you immediately have all there is in the kingdom of God. It is as deadly as cyanide. It kills all hope of spiritual advance and causes many to adopt what I call "the creed of contentment."

Why should a Christian settle down as soon as he has come to know the Lord?

I would have to reply that he must have received faulty counsel and bad exposition of New Testament truth. There is always real joy in the heart of the person who has become a child of God, and proper and sound teaching of the Word of God will awake desire within him to move forward in spiritual adventure with Christ.

But the would-be teacher may tell the new Christian, "You are now complete in Him. The Bible says that and it means that you should just be glad that you are complete and there is nothing more you will ever need!" From that time on, any effort to forge ahead for God is put down as some sort of fanaticism. This kind of exposition has brought many Christians into a place of false contentment—satisfied to stay right where they are.

But not so with the Apostle Paul who amazes and humbles us as we read in the third chapter of Philippians of his earnest desire to press forward and to become a special kind of Christian.

With great desire, he wrote: *"That I may win Christ"* (3:8)—and yet he already had Christ!

With obvious longing he said, *"That I may ... be found in Him"* (3:8-9)—and yet he was already in Him. We go to Paul more than to any other writer in the Bible to learn the doctrine of being in Christ, and yet Paul humbly and intensely breathed this great desire, *"That I may know him,"* (3:10) when he already knew Him!

It was this same Paul who gladly testified, *"I am crucified with Christ: nevertheless I live: yet not I, but Christ liveth in me: and the life which I now live in the flesh I live by the faith of the Son of God, who loved me, and gave himself for me."* (Galatians 2:20)

Yet, because he could never be standing still, he further testified, *"but I follow after, if that I may apprehend that for which also I am apprehended of Christ Jesus."* (Philippians 3:12)

How utterly foreign that is to the spirit of modern orthodoxy! How foreign to the bland assurances that because we can quote the text of Scripture, we must have the experience. This strange textualism that assumes that because we can quote chapter and verse, we possess the content and experience is a grave hindrance to spiritual progress. I think it is one of the deadliest, most chilling breezes that ever blew across the church of God!

Too many of us are complete strangers to the desire and the spirit that drove the Apostle Paul forward day by day. "That I may gain—that I may know—that I may be found in Him"—these were the words that drove Paul. But now, we are often told that we "have" everything, and that we should just be thankful and "go on to cultivate." I say that the two attitudes are foreign to one another. They do not belong together.

We are told to study the biblical passages in the Greek. We find out what they mean in English. Then we say, "Well, isn't that fine—isn't that fine!" And that is all we do about it. But Paul said, *"I press toward the mark for the prize of the high calling of God in Christ Jesus."* (Philippians 3:14)

Some have even turned that desire of Paul into a pink cloud. They believe that Paul was talking about a pink cloud, which he was going to get when Christ returned. In my opinion, there isn't anything about the return of Christ in that expression of Paul. He was talking about the present, and he was expressing his desire to continue on with Christ. He was talking about experiencing all of that for which Christ had apprehended him.

What is the Cause

Why do Christian people in our day purposely turn a deaf ear to the clear appeals in the Word of God concerning spiritual desire and victory?

In some cases, it is because they have heard truth that they are not willing to obey. Our Lord is not going to compromise with anyone over the issue of disobedience to truth that He reveals. As a result, those who knowingly refuse to obey will be brought to a distinct halt in their spiritual life. If there is something that they will not do for Him, some confession they will not make, something they refuse to straighten out, some act of obedience they will not perform—they will come to a stop and just sit. It is a dead halt—like the breaking of an axle on a truck or car.

People are sitting all around in the church of Christ, just as though the axle had broken, and they have not made any progress for years and years. They are completely stopped by nonobedience.

In other cases, Christians have been side-tracked and rendered useless by their acceptance of a state of chronic discouragement. As a result, they have come to a place of contented rationalization that their condition is normal for all Christians.

These are people who are believers, but they are not believers for themselves. They say they believe in this progressive, victorious Christian life but that it is for others, not for themselves. They have been to every altar, they have been to all of the Bible conferences, but the blessings are for someone else.

Now that attitude on the part of believers is neither modesty nor meekness. It is discouragement resulting from unbelief. It is rather like those who have been sick so long that they no longer believe they can get well. They have lived with the illness so long that it has become a pet, and they don't want to lose it because they would no longer have a subject for conversation. They would say that they want to get well, but in fact, they do not.

Jesus is still saying, as He said to the man lying by the gate at the pool, "Wilt thou be made whole?" (John 5:6). Jesus made that man whole and raised him up because he wanted to be healed and delivered. If Jesus had found in him that which He finds in so many Christians today—a chronic state of discouragement—He would have passed him by!

A third reason why many make no progress with God is the fact that they have seen fit to join the cult of respectability. They have learned the art of "becoming adjusted." They have chosen to be cool and proper, poised, self-possessed and well-rounded. They would never want anyone to think that they have taken an extreme position, particularly in religious matters.

We are getting so well-rounded and so broadly symmetrical that we forget that every superior soul that has done exploits for God was considered extreme and, in many cases, even deranged. We talk about the saintly John Wesley, a learned Oxford man and founder of the Methodists, but we forget that he was such a fiery apostle that they used to throw eggs and rocks at him. His clothes looked fine when he went out, but when he came back, he needed a tailor. Wesley never put poise and adjustment and respectability above that urgency within his soul to make Christ known with all of His saving and keeping power!

Well, thank God for the Wesleys and all the great souls who have not been afraid of being different! Thank God that there are always a few, and the Bible talks about their being worthy. I know that in Revelation 3:4 it says, *"They shall walk with me in white: for they are worthy."* I am not going to try to persuade you that I know the full meaning, but I know that even in times of backsliding and general coldness of heart, there have always been some of God's people who were different. I think there was enough difference in their love and desire and adoration that there would be no question about their walking with Him in white!

Now I wonder if any of you think that I am just trying to whip up spiritual desire in your hearts?

No, I am not trying to whip up desire for the simple reason that I know better. I can agitate you nervously, but I cannot put spiritual desire in your being.

The old saint who wrote *The Cloud of Unknowing* expressed it like this: "Our Lord hath of his great mercy called thee and led thee unto him by the desire of thine heart." I have reminded you before that God is always previous, God is always there first, and if you have any desire for God and for the things of God, it is God Himself who put it there.

That old writer continued: "Through the everlasting love of his God-head, he made thee and wrought thee when thou were not." God was already there—you didn't call up because you were not. And then, "He bought thee with the price of his precious blood when you were lost in Adam." Again, God preceded you—God was previous once more. I believe in prevenient grace, and I don't believe that any person can ever be nudged or pushed or jostled into the kingdom of God or into the deeper life except the Holy Ghost does it. He does it out of the everlasting love of His Godhead, the old saint told us, "so tenderly, he would not suffer thee to be so far from him."

Oh my brothers and sisters! Are we not stirred by the expanse of this great sea of glory in which we Christians find ourselves? "He would not suffer thee to be so far from him." He just wouldn't allow it. He just couldn't stand it. This same God who made us when we were nothing and redeemed us when we were sinners "kindled desire so graciously."

Longing For God Must Come From Him

How many of us does that describe? Have any of you ever had a gracious, sudden kindling of desire, when everyone else seemed contented with panel discussions and the usual routine of the church, which has to do with externals? How many of us go to church regularly and never feel an extra heartbeat, never any kindling of godly desire? We live like that!

So this kind of desire is not something that can be whipped up—God Himself must put it there. We could never have created ourselves, and we could never have redeemed ourselves. We cannot talk ourselves into getting a longing for God. It has to come from God.

When I was a young fellow, I spent a little time working as "butcher boy" on the train—riding the old Vicksburg and Pacific and selling peanuts, popcorn, chewing gum and candy, as well as books. I really had to quit because I didn't sell enough—I would often sit and read the books from Vicksburg to the end of the line! But I remember member that we did try to stir up some desire for peanuts and popcorn among those passengers. We would go through the coaches and give each person just four or five salted peanuts. No one wanted any when we went through, but when we came back, nearly everyone was ready to buy. They had gotten a taste and now they had a desire for peanuts. It was a common trick on the trains.

But we cannot do that for you in spiritual matters. It is not possible! If you have accepted a common state of spiritual living and you have no deep desire for Him, no man can give it to you. Unless you are willing for God to move in and have His way, you are never going to have spiritual adventures like those who have been explorers in the kingdom of God.

We don't think often enough about all those who have been the prospectors among the hills of God—the spiritual adventurers, the explorers of the kingdom. God wrote in the Bible about them because they were seeking a better land.

Why did Abraham leave Ur of the Chaldees? God promised him spiritual adventures, and he moved out at God's bidding, but it didn't make him a hero at that point.

Think of what the contented people must have said.

"Look at that fool," they said. "What's the matter with him? Everyone else is satisfied to go to the temple once a week and make an offering, but Abraham talks about hearing a voice that said 'get thee into the land which I will show thee.'"

They said, "Abraham, you are a fool!"

But Abraham said, "I heard the Voice, plain and clear. I'm moving out!"

At that point Abraham was no hero. They thought he had lost his mind, that he was at least semi-demented. But you know the rest of the story.

Then there was Moses, who could have lived on in the house of his supposed mother in Egypt and perhaps could have become the emperor. But he refused to do it. He got up and left. You know the story and the great list of his spiritual adventures and his favor with God.

Think of the apostles and all of the great souls who have been adventurers. They were not the heroes of the crowd, but they have entered into God's great Hall of Fame. But something had to happen within each one, an internal fire before it became external. This desire to prospect the hills of God for new lodes of gold had to be inward before it could be outward. These adventurers for God knew the happening on the inside before there was any evidence on the outside.

Far too many people still believe that changes on the outside will take care of the whole matter. How many there are who still think that making outward changes in life and character and habits is all that God expects. Many men have made decisions to enter the ministry or to go to work on some foreign field because of advice and pressures from the outside. That can happen to the outside of a man and never really touch his heart at all.

It can happen. It is entirely in the realm of possibility that a missionary could go to the field and spend a lifetime there and yet never have moved beyond the little patch of ground in his own spiritual life. It is not enough just to go in body, moved by something on the outside. This is a journey for the soul—not just for the feet!

This is why God wants to do something within His people. The great problem of the church today is how we may go on to experience and draw upon that which we have in Christ. But we are not doing much about the problem!

One of my preacher friends wrote me that he had been asked to help in a missionary convention in one of our churches. He was to preach on missions. He said that when he arrived, he found there had been no more spiritual preparation for those meetings than there had been for the first game of the World Series.

The first night there were about twenty-five people in attendance, but the pastor announced that a good, lively quartet would sing on the following night. My friend wrote that the church was packed. The members of the quartet exchanged jibes, lampooned one another and captured the crowd with their clowning. After singing a song that said, "Let's help God some more," and figuring, I suppose, that they had rescued God from what otherwise would have been a boring evening, they took their guitars and rushed out to another engagement to help God some more.

How will anyone grow in grace around a place like that, I ask you? It makes no difference whether it is one of our churches or some other group, or the largest cathedral in the world, no one could grow in grace in such a situation unless he had a private source. We have the

Word of God to which we can go. God has not only called us by His love but has promised a place of pasture for our spiritual good.

But some of God's dear children don't have that longing for His best pastures because in spiritual things they have not found the delight of experiencing within themselves all that Christ has provided.

I used to read from the various religions of the East and I recall a passage in the Hindu writings that said, "You who are busy learning texts and not living them are like the man counting other people's cattle without having a single heifer of his own."

I thought that was pretty good for an old Hindu, and I could translate that over into my own version and say, "A lot of professing Christians are busy counting other people's cattle—studying the theology and archaeology, anthropology and eschatology—but they don't have one little heifer of their own."

They have very little from God that is their very own. They only have that which really belongs to someone else. They might write a small tract on what God has done for them, but they could write a huge volume on all that God wants to do for them if they would consent.

God is saying, "I stand ready to pour a little liquid fire into your heart, into your spiritual being!"

We respond: "No, Lord, please excuse me. That sounds like fanaticism—and I would have to give up some things!" And so we refuse His desire, even though we want all the benefits of His cross.

There is this thoughtful phrase in *The Cloud of Unknowing*: "He wills thou do but look on Him and let Him alone." Let God alone. In other words, let Him work! Don't stop Him. Don't prevent Him from kindling your heart, from blessing you and leading you out of a common state into that of special longing after Him. You don't have to coax God. He is not like a reluctant father waiting for his child to beg. The blessings are His to give, and He waits for us to let Him work.

This is a very hard thing for Americans to do because we are naturally born "do-it-yourself" artists! We don't just hire a plumber and let him do his work—we stand by and tell him how it should be done. It is amazing really that any American ever lies down and allows the doctor to perform the operation. We always want to get our finger in, and that is the way most Christians behave. We think God does the really hard jobs, but that He is glad to have us along to help out.

"Look on Him—and let Him work, let Him alone." Get your hands down to your side and stop trying to tell God where to cut. Stop trying to make the diagnosis for God. Stop trying to tell God what to give you. He is the Physician! You are the patient.

This is good doctrine, brethren. Dr. A.B. Simpson shocked and blessed and helped dear people in all Christian groups as he taught his truth down through the years—"Let God work! Let Him alone! Take your hands off! It is God that worketh in you!"

Let Him work and your spiritual life will begin to blaze like the rising sun.

27.Thinking of Time As Powerful

Sin has done frightful things to us and its effect upon us is all the more deadly because we were born in it and are scarcely aware of what is happening to us.

One thing sin has done is to confuse our values so that we can only with difficulty distinguish a friend from a foe or tell for certain what is and what is not good for us. We walk in a world of shadows where real things appear unreal and things of no consequence are sought after as eagerly as if they were made of the very gold that paves the streets of the City of God.

Our ideas rarely accord with things as they are, but are distorted by a kind of moral astigmatism that throws everything out of focus. Through a multitude of errors our total philosophy is out of line, somewhat as our mathematics would be had we learned the multiplication table wrongly and not been aware of our mistake.

One false concept to which we cling tenaciously is time. We think of it as being a sort of viscid substance flowing onward like a sluggish river, bearing upon its bosom nations and empires and civilizations and men. We visualize this sticky stream as an entity and ourselves as helplessly stuck in it for as long as our earthly lives endure.

Or again, by a simple shift in our thinking we picture time as a revealer of the shape of things to come, as when we say, "Time will tell." Or we imagine it a benign physician and comfort ourselves with the thought, "Time is a great healer." All this is so much a part of us that it would be too much to expect that the habit of referring everything to time could never be broken. Yet we may guard against the harm that such thinking carries with it.

The most harmful mistake we make concerning time is that it has somehow a mysterious power to perfect human nature. We say of a foolish young man, "Time will make him wiser," or we see a new Christian acting like anything but a Christian and hope that time will someday turn him into a saint.

The truth is that time has no more power to sanctify a man than space has. Indeed time is only a fiction by which we account for change. It is change, not time, that turns fools into wise men and sinners into saints. Or more accurately, it is Christ who does the whole thing by means of the changes He works in the heart.

Saul the persecutor became Paul the servant of God, but time did not make the change. Christ wrought the miracle, the same Christ who once changed water into wine. One spiritual experience followed another in fairly rapid succession until the violent Saul became a gentle, God-enamored soul ready to lay down his life for the faith he once hated. It should be obvious that time had no part in the making of the man of God.

My purpose in writing this little piece is not to engage in an exercise in semantics but to alert my readers to the injury they may suffer from an unfounded confidence in time. Because a Moses and a Jacob lost the impulsive, headstrong sins of their youth and in their old age became gentle, mellow saints we tend to take it for granted that time wrought the transformation. But it is not so. God, not time, makes saints.

Human nature is not fixed, and for this we should thank God day and night. We are still capable of change. We can become something other than what we are. By the power of the gospel the covetous man may become generous, the egotist lowly in his own eyes. The thief may learn to steal no more, the blasphemer to fill his mouth with praises unto God. But it is Christ who does it all. Time has nothing to do with it.

Many a lost man is putting off the day of salvation, vaguely hoping that time is on his side, when actually the likelihood of his ever becoming a Christian grows less day by day. And why? Because the changes taking place in him are hardening his will and making it more and more difficult for him to repent.

"Seek ye the LORD while he may be found, call ye upon him while he is near: Let the wicked forsake his way, and the unrighteous man his thoughts: and let him return unto the LORD, and he will have mercy upon him; and to our God, for he will abundantly pardon." (Isaiah 55:6–7)

See the change-words in this text: "seek ... call ... forsake ... return." These all denote specific changes the returning sinner must make in himself, acts that he must perform. But this is not enough. "Have mercy ... pardon"; these are the changes God makes in and for the man. To be saved the man must change and be changed.

To enter the kingdom of God, our Lord explained, a man must be born again (John 3:3–7). That is, he must undergo a spiritual change. This accords completely with the preaching of John the Baptist who called upon his hearers to prepare the way of the Lord by bringing forth fruits worthy of repentance, and with the apostle Peter who reminded the early Christians that they had been made partakers of the divine nature and had escaped the corruption the world had suffered by lust.

The initial change, however, is not the only one the redeemed man will know. His whole Christian life will consist of a succession of changes, moving always toward spiritual perfection. To achieve these changes the Holy Spirit uses various means, probably the most effective being the writing of the New Testament.

Time can help us only if we know that it cannot help us at all. It is change we need, and only God can change us from worse to better.

28.Utilitarian View of Christ

Our Lord forewarned us that false Christs should come. Mostly we think of these as coming from the outside, but we should remember that they may also arise within the sanctuary itself.

We must be extremely careful that the Christ we profess to follow is indeed the very Christ of God. There is always danger that we may be following a Christ who is not the true Christ but one conjured up by our imagination and made in our own image.

I confess to a feeling of uneasiness about this when I observe the questionable things Christ is said to do for people these days. He is often recommended as a wonderfully obliging but not too discriminating Big Brother who delights to help us to accomplish our ends, and who further favors us by forbearing to ask any embarrassing questions about the moral and spiritual qualities of those ends.

In our eagerness to lead men to "accept Christ", we are often tempted to present for acceptance a Christ who is little more than a caricature of "that holy thing" which was conceived by the Holy Ghost, born of the Virgin Mary, to be crucified and rise the third day to take His place on the right hand of the Majesty in the heavens.

Within the past few years, for instance, Christ has been popularized by some so-called evangelicals as one who, if a proper amount of prayer were made, would help the pious prizefighter to knock another fighter unconscious in the ring. Christ is also said to help the big-league pitcher to get the proper hook on his curve.

In another instance He assists an athletically minded person to win the high jump, and still another not only to come in first in a track meet, but also to set a new record in the bargain. He is said also to have helped a praying businessman to beat out a competitor in a deal, to underbid a rival and to secure a coveted contract to the discomfiture of someone else who was trying to get it. He is even thought to lend succor to a praying movie actress while she plays a role so lewd as to bring blood to the face of a professional prostitute.

Thus, our Lord becomes the Christ of utility, a kind of Aladdin's lamp to do minor miracles on behalf of anyone who summons Him to do his bidding.

Apparently, no one stops to consider that if Christ were to step into a prize ring and use His divine power to help one prizefighter to paralyze another, He would be putting one fighter at a cruel disadvantage and violating every common instinct of fair play. If He were to aid one businessman to the detriment of another, He would be practicing favoritism and revealing a character wholly unlike the Bible picture of the real Christ. Furthermore, we would have the grotesque situation of the Lord of glory coming to the aid of an unreconstructed Adam—on Adam's terms.

All this is too horrible to contemplate, and I hope that the proponents of this modern accommodating Christ do not see the implications that lie in their shoddy doctrine. But perhaps they do see, and are willing nevertheless to offer this utilitarian Christ as the Savior of mankind. If so, then they no longer believe in the deity of the lordship of Christ in any proper definition of those words. Theirs is a Christ of carnal convenience, not too far removed from the gods of paganism.

The whole purpose of God in redemption is to make us holy and to restore us to the image of God. To accomplish this, He disengages us from earthly ambitions and draws us away from the cheap and unworthy prizes that worldly men set their hearts upon. A holy man would not dream of asking God to help him beat an opponent or win over a competitor. He would not wish to succeed if to do so another man must fail. No man in whom the Spirit dwells could bring himself to ask the Lord to help him knock another man unconscious for filthy lucre or the plaudits of the vulgar spectators.

A Joshua fighting the battles of the Lord, a David rescuing God's Israel from the Philistines, a Washington seeking God's help against the enemy that would enslave the young America—this is up on a high level of moral and spiritual principle and in line with the purpose of God in human history. But to teach that Christ will use His sacred power to further our worldly interests is to wrong our Lord and injure our own souls. We modern evangelicals need to learn the truths of the sovereignty of God and the lordship of Christ. God will not play along with Adam; Christ will not be used by any of Adam's selfish brood. We had better learn these things fast if this generation of young Christians is to be spared the supreme tragedy of following a Christ who is merely a Christ of convenience and not the true Lord of glory after all.

29.Disparity Between Theology and Practice

There is an evil which I have seen under the sun and which in its effect upon the Christian religion may be more destructive than communism, Romanism and liberalism combined. It is the glaring disparity between theology and practice among professing Christians.

So wide is the gulf that separates theory from practice in the Church that an inquiring stranger who chances upon both would scarcely dream that there was any relation between them. An intelligent observer of our human scene who heard the Sunday morning sermon and later watched the Sunday afternoon conduct of those who had heard it would conclude that he had been examining two distinct and contrary religions.

A church conference, for instance, may listen to and applaud the most spiritual message, and twenty minutes later adopt the most carnal procedure, altogether as if they had not heard the impassioned moral appeal a few moments before. Christians habitually weep and pray over beautiful truth, only to draw back from that same truth when it comes to the difficult job of putting it in practice.

The average church simply does not dare to check its practices against biblical precepts. It tolerates things that are diametrically opposed to the will of God, and if the matter is pointed out to its leaders, they will defend its unscriptural practices with a smooth casuistry equal to the verbal dodging of the Roman moralists.

This can be explained only by assuming a lack of integration in the religious personality. There seems to be no vital connection between the emotional and volitional departments of the life. The mind can approve and the emotions enjoy while the will drags its feet and refuses to go along. And since Christ makes His appeal directly to the will, are we not justified in wondering whether or not these divided souls have ever made a true committal to the Lord? Or whether they have been inwardly renewed?

It appears that too many Christians want to enjoy the thrill of feeling right, but are not willing to endure the inconvenience of being right.

So, the divorce between theory and practice becomes permanent in fact, though in word the union is declared to be eternal. Truth sits forsaken and grieves till her professed followers come home for a brief visit, but she sees them depart again when the bills become due. They protest great and undying love for her but they will not let their love cost them anything.

Could this be the condition our Lord had in mind when He said, *"Thou hast a name that thou livest, and art dead"* (Revelation 3:1)? What can the effect be upon the spectators who live day after day among professed Christians who habitually ignore the commandments of Christ and live after their own private notions of Christianity? Will they not conclude that the whole thing is false? Will they not be forced to believe that the faith of Christ is an unreal and visionary thing which they are fully justified in rejecting?

Certainly, the non-Christian is not too much to be blamed if he turns disgustedly away from the invitation of the gospel after he has been exposed for a while to the inconsistencies of those of his acquaintances who profess to follow Christ. The deadening effect of religious make-believe on the human mind is beyond all describing.

In that great and terrible day when the deeds of men are searched into by the penetrating eyes of the Judge of all the earth, what will we answer when we are charged with inconsistency and moral fraud? And at whose door will lie the blame for the millions of lost men who while they lived on earth were sickened and revolted by the religious travesty they knew as Christianity?

30. Contentment With our Spiritual State

One of the big milk companies makes capital of the fact that their cows are all satisfied with their lot in life. Their clever ads have made the term "contented cows" familiar to everyone. But what is a virtue in a cow may be a vice in a man. And contentment, when it touches spiritual things, is surely a vice.

Paul professed that he had learned to be content with such earthly good as fell to his lot. That is something else from being content with his spiritual attainments. With these he specifically declared that he was not satisfied:

Brethren, I count not myself to have apprehended: but this one thing I do, forgetting those things which are behind, and reaching forth unto those things which are before, I press toward the mark for the prize of the high calling of God in Christ Jesus. (Philippians 3:13–14)

Contentment with earthly goods is the mark of a saint; contentment with our spiritual state is a mark of inward blindness.

One of the greatest fears of the Christian is religious complacency. The man who believes he has arrived will not go any farther; from his standpoint it would be foolish to do so. The snare is to believe we have arrived when we have not. The present neat habit of quoting a text to prove we have arrived may be a dangerous one if in truth we have no actual inward experience of the text. Truth that is not experienced is no better than error and may be fully as dangerous. The scribes who sat in Moses' seat were not the victims of error; they were the victims of their failure to experience the truth they taught.

Religious complacency is encountered almost everywhere among Christians these days, and its presence is a sign and a prophecy. For every Christian will become at last what his desires have made him. We are all the sum total of our hungers.

The great saints have all had thirsting hearts. Their cry has been, "*My soul thirsteth for God, for the living God: when shall I come and appear before God?*" (Psalm 42:2). Their longing after God all but consumed them. It propelled them onward and upward to heights toward which less ardent Christians look with languid eye and entertain no hope of reaching.

Orthodox Christianity has fallen to its present low estate from lack of spiritual desire. Among the many who profess the Christian faith, scarcely one in a thousand reveals any passionate thirst for God. The practice of many of our spiritual advisers is to use the Scriptures to discourage such little longing as may be discovered here and there among us. We fear extremes and shy away from too much ardor in religion, as if it were possible to have too much love or too much faith or too much holiness.

Occasionally one's heart is cheered by the discovery of some insatiable saint who is willing to sacrifice everything for the sheer joy of experiencing God in increasing intimacy. To such we offer this word of exhortation: Pray on, fight on, sing on. Do not underrate anything God may have done for you heretofore. Thank God for everything up to this point, but do not stop here. Press on into the deep things of God. Insist upon tasting the profounder mysteries of redemption. Keep your feet on the ground, but let your heart soar as high as it will. Refuse to be average or to surrender to the chill of your spiritual environment.

If you thus "follow after," heaven will surely be opened to you and you will, with Ezekiel, see visions of God.

Unless you do these things you will reach at last (and unknown to you) the bone yard of orthodoxy and be doomed to live out your days in a spiritual state which can be best described as "the dead level and quintessence of every mediocrity."

From such a state God save us all.

31.Lowering Our Guard

Someday the Church can relax her guard, call her watchmen down from the wall and live in safety and peace; but not yet, not yet.

All that is good in the world stands as a target for all that is evil and manages to stay alive only by constant watchfulness and the providential protection of Almighty God. As a man or a nation may be in deepest trouble when unaware of any trouble at all and in gravest danger when ignorant that any danger exists, so the church may be in greatest peril by not recognizing the presence of peril or the source from which it comes.

The church at Laodicea has stood for 1,900 years as a serious warning to the whole Church of Christ to be most watchful when no enemy is in sight and to remain poor in spirit when earthly wealth increases, yet we appear to have learned nothing from her. We expound the seven letters to the churches of Asia and then return to our own company to live like the Laodicean church. There is in us a bent to back-sliding that is all but impossible to cure.

The healthiest man has enough lethal bacteria in him to kill him within twenty-four hours except for one thing—the amazing power of the human organism to resist bacterial attack. Every mortal body must fight its internal enemies day and night. Once it surrenders, its hours are numbered. Quite literally it must fight or die.

The reason for this is that the human race inhabits a fallen world which is in many ways hostile to it. Nature as well as man is fallen; and as sin is normal human powers gone astray, so disease results from microscopic creatures once meant to be useful to men but now out of hand and perverted. To live, the body must resist these invisible enemies successfully, and considering our high vulnerability and the number of our enemies it is wonderful that any of us manages to live beyond his childhood.

The Church lives in a hostile world. Within and around her are enemies that not only could destroy her, but are meant to and will, unless she resists force with yet greater force. The Christian would collapse from sheer external pressure were there not within him a counterpressure sufficiently great to prevent it. The power of the Holy Spirit is, therefore, not optional but necessary. Without it the children of God simply cannot live the life of heaven on earth. The hindrances are too many and too effective.

A Church is a living organism and is subject to attack from such enemies as prey on living things. Yet the figure of the human body to stand for the Church is not adequate, for the life of the body is non-intelligent, whereas the Church is composed of moral beings having intelligence to recognize their enemies and a will to enable them to resist. The human body can fight its enemies even while it is asleep, but the Church cannot. She must be awake and determined or she cannot win.

One enemy we must resist is *unbelief.* The temptation is strong to reject what we cannot explain, or at least to withhold belief till we have investigated further. This attitude is proper, even commendable, for the scientist, but wholly wrong for the Christian. Here is the reason:

The faith of the Christian rests down squarely upon the man Christ Jesus who declares that He is both God and Lord. This claim must be received by pure faith or rejected outright; it can never be proved by investigation. That is why Christ's appeal is directed to faith alone. The believer thinks, it is true; but he thinks because he believes, not in order that he may. Faith secures from the indwelling Spirit confirmation exquisitely perfect, but only after it is there without other support than Christ Himself.

Another enemy is *complacency.* "Woe to them that are at ease in Zion" (Amos 6:1). The contented Christian is not in danger of attack, he has already been attacked. He is sick and does not know it. To escape this we must stir up the gift of God which is in us. We must declare war on contentment and press toward the mark for the prize of the high calling of God in Christ Jesus.

Again, there is *self-righteousness.* The temptation to feel morally pleased with ourselves will be all the greater as our lives become better. The only sure defense against this is to cultivate a quiet state of continual penitence. A sweet but sobering memory of our past guilt and a knowledge of our present imperfections are not incompatible with the joy of the Lord; and they are of inestimable aid in resisting the enemy.

The fear of man brings a snare, said the prophet, and this enemy too must be defeated. Our whole modern world is geared to destroy individual independence and bring all of us into conformity to all the rest of us. Any deviation from the pattern, whatever that pattern may be at the time, will not be forgiven by society, and since the Christian must deviate radically from the world he naturally comes in for the world's displeasure. If he surrenders to fear he has been conquered, and he dare not let this happen.

Other enemies maybe identified, such as *love of luxury, secret sympathy with the world, self-confidence, pride* and *unholy thoughts.* These we must resist with every power within us, looking unto Jesus, the author and finisher of our faith.

32. The Dead Hope of The Second Coming

Shortly after the close of the first World War, I heard a great Southern preacher say that he feared the intense interest in prophecy, which was current at that time, would result in a dying out of the blessed hope when events had proved the excited interpreters wrong.

The man was a prophet or at least a remarkably shrewd student of human nature, for exactly what he predicted has come to pass. The hope of Christ's coming is today all but dead among evangelicals.

I do not mean that Bible Christians have given up the doctrine of the second advent. By no means. There has been, as every informed person knows, an adjustment among some of the lesser tenets of our prophetic credo, but the vast majority of evangelicals continue to hold to the belief that Jesus Christ will sometime actually come back to the earth in person. The ultimate triumph of Christ is accepted as one of the unshakable doctrines of Holy Scripture.

It is true that in some quarters the prophecies of the Bible are occasionally expounded. This is especially so among Hebrew Christians who, for reasons well understood, seem to feel closer to the prophets of the Old Testament than do Gentile believers.

Their love for their own people naturally leads them to grasp at every hope of the conversion and ultimate restoration of Israel. To many of them the return of Christ represents a quick and happy solution of the "Jewish problem." The long centuries of wandering will end when He comes and God will at that time "restore again the kingdom to Israel."

We dare not allow our deep love for our Hebrew Christian brethren to blind us to the obvious political implications of this aspect of their Messianic hope. We do not blame them for this. We merely call attention to it.

Yet the return of Christ as a blessed hope is, as I have said, all but dead among us. The truth touching the second advent, where it is presented today, is for the most part either academic or political. The joyful personal element is altogether missing. Where are they who

"*Yearn for the sign, O Christ, of thy fulfilling,*

Faint for the flaming of Thine advent feet"?

The longing to see Christ that burned in the breasts of those first Christians seems to have burned itself out. All we have left are the ashes. It is precisely the "yearning" and the "fainting" for the return of Christ that has distinguished the personal hope from the theological one. Mere acquaintance with correct doctrine is a poor substitute for Christ, and familiarity with New Testament eschatology will never take the place of a love-inflamed desire to look on His face.

If the tender yearning is gone from the advent hope today, there must be a reason for it. And I think I know what it is, or what they are, for there are a number of them.

One is simply that popular fundamentalist theology has emphasized the utility of the cross, rather than the beauty of the One who died on it. The saved man's relation to Christ has been made contractual instead of personal.

The "work" of Christ has been stressed until it has eclipsed the person of Christ. Substitution has been allowed to supersede identification. What He did for me seems to be more important than what He is to me. Redemption is seen as an across-the-counter transaction which we "accept," and the whole thing lacks emotional content. We must love someone very much to stay awake and long for his coming, and that may explain the absence of power in the advent hope even among those who still believe in it.

Another reason for the absence of real yearning for Christ's return is that Christians are so comfortable in this world that they have little desire to leave it. For those leaders who set the pace of religion and determine its content and quality, Christianity has become of late remarkably lucrative. The streets of gold do not have too great an appeal for those who find it so easy to pile up gold and silver in the service of the Lord here on earth.

We all want to reserve the hope of heaven as a kind of insurance against the day of death, but as long as we are healthy and comfortable, why exchange a familiar good for something about which we actually know very little? Thus reasons the carnal mind, and so subtly that we are scarcely aware of it.

Again, in these times religion has become jolly good fun right here in this present world, and what's the hurry about heaven anyway? Christianity, contrary to what some had thought, is another and higher form of entertainment. Christ has done all the suffering. He has shed all the tears and carried all the crosses. We have but to enjoy the benefits of His heartbreak in the form of religious pleasures modeled after the world but carried on in the name of Jesus. So say the same people who claim to believe in Christ's second coming.

History reveals that times of suffering for the Church have also been times of looking upward. Tribulation has always sobered God's people and encouraged them to look for and yearn after the return of their Lord. Our present preoccupation with this world may be a warning of bitter days to come. God will wean us from the earth some way—the easy way if possible, the hard way if necessary. It is up to us.

33. The Judge and Savior

For as the Father hath life in himself;

so hath he given to the Son to have life in himself;

And hath given him authority to execute judgment also,

because he is the Son of man.

JOHN 5:22-29

It is only because of the Incarnation that God in His wisdom and grace can bring all of humanity to a point of accountability. This is something we can both rejoice over and be fearful of, and it enables God to bring all of humanity to His judgment bar.

No matter where you go in the world, you will run into the concept of judgment, with variations in detail. The basic concept of judgment is simply that human beings are morally accountable. The basis of this accountability is the fact that we have life derived from another and not from ourselves.

Because our life has come from another, we have a moral responsibility to that one who gave us life. The Father, so the Scriptures teach us, has life in Himself; therefore, nobody can judge the father. God is not a derived; He is the original. Furthermore, the Scripture says, *"For as the Father hath life in himself; so hath he given to the Son to have life in himself,"* (John 5:26) so no one can judge the Son. The Son is of the Father alone. Out of this comes the concept of universal judgment. While we are free to make moral choices, we are nevertheless under necessity to account for some authority for those choices.

I have used a word and a phrase— "free" and "under necessity"—and one seems to cancel the other out. But there is nothing inconsistent here. Men are free to decide their own moral choices, but they are also under the necessity to account to God for those choices. That makes them both free and bound, for they are bound to come to judgment and to give account for the deeds done in the body.

In Ralph Waldo Emerson's famous essay, he develops the idea that there is no such thing as a future judgment. Everything is judged and sentenced and rewarded or punished now. To illustrate this, he said, "The thief only steals from himself." This of course is not the universal belief, and it is not the belief of the Old Testament, nor is it the teaching of the New Testament, nor the teaching of the Church. It was hatched out of the head of the great man who lived in Concord, Massachusetts.

As anyone might expect, there are many wrong and inadequate concepts of Judgment judgment. Again, wherever you have two or three gathered together you will have at least two or three concepts of judgment. It is like the Old Testament Scripture that said, "Every man did that which was right in his own eyes" (Judg. 17:6). Let me name a few concepts of judgment that are popular but inadequate.

The first concept is the operation of the law of compensation. I take something out of my left pocket and I put it in my right pocket. Everything you do in one direction has to be counterbalanced by something in the opposite direction.

Another inadequate concept of judgment is that we are accountable only to society. Certainly, there is a world of truth in this, but it's only part truth. When we do something against society, we are accountable to society. But we are also responsible to God and accountable to Him for our actions.

Much of this has to do with public opinion. Public opinion is what judges you and indeed has already judged the things you do. Proof of what I'm saying was brought home to me a few years ago. I was walking down the street when a little boy took a good look at me as I walked along. Usually I am friendly to children, but I was preoccupied that day, and when I got within hearing distance of him, he looked up at me and said, "Hello, pickle puss." He had me figured out already. I was a pickle puss, and I was responsible to human society for the very shape my face was in. I was not mad at anybody, but he evidently thought I was not as cheerful looking as I might have been. He thought he would needle me a little, which he did. So we are responsible to society for everything we do.

There are many ways in which we are accountable to public opinion. Simply driving down the highway causes people to conclude that you are either a good driver and a good person or you are a road hog—one or the other. Your neighbors will judge you as a good neighbor or a bad neighbor based on public opinion.

Another inadequate concept of judgment is that we are accountable to human law. From the most primitive tribes in New Guinea to the most civilized culture in London or New York or Paris, every nation establishes laws. Those nations expect those laws to be respected and abided by, or suffer the consequences.

Somebody may point out the lawbreaker. Here is a person who breaks the law in order to get money. He may rob a bank so that he might get money to pay his taxes or pay something else. But he is keeping one law and breaking another law to get the money to do it. So, the outlaw is an outlaw only in certain details; he keeps the majority of the laws but breaks one law for personal profit or convenience.

An outlaw is never a happy man because he is accountable to the law even while he is breaking it, and he is miserable even while he is flaunting the law.

There is another inadequate concept of judgment, and that is that man's accountability is to himself alone. According to this concept, each and every person stands before the bar of his own reason and of his own conscience, which would be the judge and jury.

The basis of this is the idea of relativity of morals and is being taught in many of our universities today. Simply put, it is that each man is a law unto himself. Nothing is really bad or good. Good is whatever brings social approval, and bad is whatever brings social disapproval. Something may be good today and tomorrow it might be evil.

This is probably the worst concept of judgment in all of society. Because if it is true, then there would be as many moral codes as there are human beings, and each would be his own witness, prosecutor, judge, jury and jailer. That is so silly it is scarcely worth any consideration.

I never underestimate the ability of man to get things mixed up. Anyone with an eloquent manner can convince people to believe anything. This of course is the core of all the cults that have sprung up throughout the years. Let me ask this question. How can a man be accountable to himself? If this is true, then how does it play out?

Someone might say, "He's accountable to his conscience." And I can see the argument here. But then my question is, to whom is his conscience accountable? How in the world can I be my own prosecutor, my own witness on the prosecuting side, my own prosecuting attorney, my own judge, my own jailer and my own executioner? I know it sounds quite learned and mystical and very poetic and dreamy, but when you consider it, it is simply ridiculous. It is an absolutely inadequate concept of judgment, for I never knew anybody to be hard on himself—to stand as judge and jury of himself and punish himself. Most people are very easy on themselves. I know if I were to be my judge, jury, prosecutor and executioner, I think I would lose my axe. I certainly would not cut off my own head. I would not have the courage to do it.

Understanding God as He is revealed in the Scriptures, it is quite clear that God is not going to make men ultimately accountable to self. And to take this further, neither is he going to make you and me ultimately accountable to the law or human society. We are accountable finally, and ultimately, to the One who gave us life. We are accountable to God alone. I believe it is the absence of this that makes soft, spineless Christians and churches without any meaning in them at all.

The simple truth is, society cannot reach us in that sphere of our being where we are most vitally accountable to God and to ourselves. As a human being and an American, I am accountable to public opinion, and I am accountable to the law of the land. But I am also accountable to myself and to my God; and human society cannot touch me there. The laws of the land and public opinion only go so far. There is truth in them, but not the entire truth. There is something beyond all of this.

Take for example a man who commits suicide. Say he takes a gun, turns the gun on his head and blows out his brains. At that point he is not accountable to public opinion or to the law of the land. He is gone beyond that and he now is accountable to a higher authority, because once he dies, the society cannot punish him.

There are many things society and the law of the land cannot deal with. Jesus understood this when He said, "Ye have heard that it was said by them of old time, Thou shalt not commit adultery: But I say unto you, That whosoever looketh on a woman to lust after her hath committed adultery with her already in his heart" (Matt. 5:27-28). The Jewish law could deal with adultery, but when it came to lust of the heart, the law could not touch it.

This kind of nonsense has even invaded our churches. Whenever a church backslides from the truth and runs away from the plain Word of God, that church begins establishing its own laws. One church I heard of, that once was a solid Bible-preaching church, advertised that on a certain Sunday morning the topic of the good Reverend's sermon was going to be on peptic ulcers. Now, what that has to do with the Bible and going on with God baffles my imagination. If I hung around that congregation for long, I probably would develop a peptic ulcer myself. It is amazing what depths we fall to and what fools we become when we become a law unto ourselves.

In the city of Detroit some years ago, the sign out front of a church announced that next Sunday morning at 10:45 A.M., the Reverend Doctor would preach on the theme, "Who Killed Cock Robin." How the good Reverend knew who the culprit was is anybody's guess.

An anonymous ancient proverb says, "Those whom the gods wish to destroy they first make mad." The judgment of God will begin to fall on the church. When they cease to believe in the judgment of God, you never know what that church will get into next or where it will go. It was belief in the accountability of man to his Maker that made America great at one time.

One of the great leaders of America was Daniel Webster. That great bulging brow of his and those blazing eyes used to hold the Senate spellbound as he stood there and talked to them not with silly quips or funny remarks. The Senate in those days was not composed of half-baked comedians but of strong, noble statesmen who carried the weight of the nation on their shoulders.

Someone said, "Mr. Webster, what do you consider the most serious thought that has ever entered your mind?" He said, "The most solemn thought that has ever entered my mind is the accountability to my Maker."

Men who talked like that could not be corrupted and bought off. And they would not have to be ashamed to have their telephone calls read back to them. They were not worried about what people thought so much as the fact that they were accountable to God.

In order for someone to judge humanity certain criteria need to be put in Judge place. Not just anybody can do this. Along with this, he must have authority to execute the judgment that is needed. Another criterion would be that the ones being so judged must be accountable to the judge. Some kind of relationship needs to be established.

Out in the world, a group of men may establish a law, as in our country over 200 years ago. People are being judged today based upon the laws established then, but not really knowing the people who established those laws. This is not the way it is in the kingdom of God. To be a judge, according to the Scripture, the judge judges those who are accountable to Him. Accountable not only by law imposed by another, but accountable morally and vitally rather than merely legally. In order to be a righteous judge of mankind, the judge has to have a variety of qualities or attributes.

The judge that we have to do with has all knowledge. He is all knowing without any exception. In order for this judge to judge rightly, there is no room for error. In our judicial system, many judges have made errors because they did not have all the facts before them. Human justice does its best, but because it is not all wise, it makes mistakes. There are some in prison today who are serving lifetime sentences that because of a mistake are in prison.

But when we come to God Almighty, He is never going to judge anybody with only partial information. God does not make mistakes; neither does He allow any error or lack of information come into the situation. This judge that judges us must be one who has all wisdom; therefore, we must eliminate Paul the apostle, Moses the lawgiver and even Elijah. These were good men but they were men only and had only finite knowledge and wisdom. The God who judges us is the judge who has infinite wisdom and is all knowing.

When it comes to judging a soul that will live for all eternity, there is no room allowed for mistakes. The judge of humanity is going to have to be one that will never need the testimony of a third party. Today they bring witnesses in and the judge sits solemnly and listens to the testimony. The witness says, "I saw him do this, I heard him say that," and if the witness is lying, the judge is misled. But the judge of mankind is not dependent upon the testimony of another.

Christ says, *"I can of mine own self do nothing: as I hear, I judge: and my judgment is just; because I seek not mine own will, but the will of the Father which hath sent me."* (John 5:30)

The basic criterion to judge all of humanity is perfect and complete knowledge.

Another criterion plays into this. The judge must be absolutely impartial and disinterested, without any personal interest in the case whatsoever. Many a judge has been severe in judgments because election time was coming up or because public opinion was getting strong. The newspapers were getting on him, and to save his political career, he passed a severe sentence or did not pass a sentence. His motives were ulterior and false. The Son of God says that His judgment is just because He does not seek His own will, but the will of the Father. Christ can be the judge because He is personally related and yet disinterested, with nothing to gain or lose by His judgment. But all the glory belongs to God.

Another important criterion to qualify the judge is a sympathetic understanding. Personally, I do not want to be judged by some archangel that never shed a tear. Nor do I want to be judged by a seraphim that never felt pain. I do not want to be judged by a cherub that never knew human grief or disappointment or woe.

For the judge to be the judge of humanity, He must be one of them. Jesus said, the Father hath given the Son power to execute judgment because He is a Son of man. Because He is a Son of man, He not only can be their advocate above, the Savior by the throne of love, but He can also be their judge to sit upon the throne.

With that in place, it eliminates all false accusations. Then there will be no dodging, no whimpering, no whining, no crying on our wrists and saying, "But Lord, You didn't understand." He does understand, because He became one of us and walked among us. Never was a tear He did not share; never a bitter disappointment He did not feel; never a grief He did not suffer; never a temptation that did not come to Him; never a critical situation that He was not in.

This brings us to the ultimate judge of all humanity, the one who alone qualifies, and none other. This one is Jesus Christ. Because He is the Son of man, He has authority to execute judgment. Christ qualifies on every count to be the judge of humanity. The tears that He shed, the pains that He suffered and the grief He bore made Him not only a just but a sympathetic judge of humanity. Now His presence in the human race is our present judgment on sin.

"And Jesus said, For judgment I am come into this world, that they which see not might see; and that they which see might be made blind." (John 9:39)

There are many Judge doctrines, important doctrines, neglected by the Bible teachers of today. This would be one of those doctrines:

Jesus Christ is the judge of mankind, but the Father judges no man.

"When the Son of man shall come in his glory, and all the holy angels with him, then shall he sit upon the throne of his glory: And before him shall be gathered all nations: and he shall separate them one from another, as a shepherd divideth his sheep from the goats." (Matt. 25:31-32)

It is He who is the judge, and when the judge of humanity shall appear, He will have the shoulders of a man and the face of a man, the man Christ Jesus. God has given Him authority to judge mankind so that He is both the judge and the Savior of man. That makes me both love Him and fear Him; love Him because He is my Savior, and fear Him because He is my judge.

Unfortunately, the ten-cent-store Jesus being preached now by many men is not the Jesus that will come to judge the world. This plastic, painted Christ who has no spine and no justice, but is a soft and pliant friend to everybody, if He is the only Christ, then we might as well close our books, bar our doors and make a bakery or garage out of our church buildings.

The popular Christ being preached now is not the Christ of God nor the Christ of the Bible nor the Christ we must deal with finally. For the Christ that we deal with has eyes as a flame of fire. And His feet are like burnished brass; and out of His mouth cometh a sharp two-edged sword (see Rev. 1:14-16). He will be the judge of humanity. You can leave your loved ones in His hands knowing that He Himself suffered, knowing that He knows all, no mistakes can be made, there can be no miscarriage of justice, because He knows all that can be known.

It was said one time as an afterthought that Jesus need not that any should testify of man, for He knew what was in man. *"Marvel not at this: for the hour is coming, in the which all that are in the graves shall hear his voice, And shall come forth; they that have done good, unto the resurrection of life; and they that have done evil, unto the resurrection of damnation."*

(John 5:28-29)

This coming out of the grave will be at the invitation of the Son of God Himself. Like an army file officer, He will command and they will stand on their feet, a great army to receive judgment, and the judgment will be based strangely enough upon the kind of life they lived in this world. That is another forgotten doctrine, but it is here. They that have done good, unto the resurrection of life; they that have done evil, unto the resurrection of damnation. And this is the judge of all.

Jesus Christ our Lord, the judge with the flaming eyes, is the one with whom we must deal. We cannot escape it. They can shrug Him off and drive away in a cloud of fumes, but everyone must come back and deal with Him finally. Be sure of one thing, He will either be Savior now or judge then. And the tenderness and sympathy of the Savior now will be laid aside while the justice and severity of the judge comes to the front. Without canceling out one, He will exercise both. So that Jesus Christ is both the Lord and the judge of men as well as the Savior of men.

Isaac Watts, in his hymn "Not All the Blood of Beasts," illustrates this very truth:

Not all the blood of beasts

On Jewish altars slain

Could give the guilty conscience peace

Or wash away the stain.

But Christ, the heav'nly Lamb,

Takes all our sins away;

A sacrifice of nobler name

And richer blood than they.

My faith would lay her hand

On that dear head of Thine,

While, like a penitent, I stand,

And there confess my sin.

My soul looks back to see

The burdens Thou didst bear

When hanging on the cursed tree,

And knows her guilt was there.

Believing, we rejoice

To see the curse remove;

We bless the Lamb with cheerful voice,

And sing his bleeding love.

In the Old Testament, the sinner would come to the priest and say, "I have sinned and I bring a lamb," or some other offering. They would take that creature and the sinner would lay his hand on the head of the beast and they would kill it and sprinkle its blood; and the sin that he had committed would be forgiven him.

Those of you who do not want Jesus as a judge, you had better think seriously now about Him as a Savior and stand like a penitent or kneel like one and confess your sin. "My soul looks back to see the burdens thou didst bare when hanging on the cursed tree and knows her guilt was there." Do you believe that your guilt was there in that cursed tree? He that knew no sin became sin for us that we might become the righteousness of God in Him (see 2 Cor. 5:21), and then Watts's hymn says, "Believing, we rejoice to see the curse remove" (see Gal. 3:13-14).

I have seen this song edited and twisted around; some educated, sophisticated editor who did not like this word "curse" removed it. He fixed it up, but I will not sing it. I sing this one: "Believing, we rejoice to see the curse remove." What curse? The curse of the broken law. The curse of sin.

"We bless the Lamb with cheerful voice and sing His bleeding love." How wonderful all this is! What a wonderful song of triumph! What a song full of theology and meaning and gospel. What the blood of goats could not do, the blood of Christ is doing and has done.

Which is He going to be for you: Savior or Judge? He will be one or the other. If He is the first, He will not be the second. But if He is not the Savior, He will be the Judge. I, for my part, cannot afford to face Him as my Judge. I must have His protecting blood and face Him as my Savior now. He knows too much about me for me to brazenly barge into His presence and let Him judge me.

The Scriptures tell us of certain ones that have sent their sins on before the judgment. You can send your sins on before the judgment, having judged, settled and dispelled them now while you are still on the earth. The Savior will cover your sins. As the old brother said, "If Jesus Christ had covered our sins with His life when they took His life away, they had been exposed but He covered them with His death. And by His death forever, He put my sins where they cannot be found, for the blood of the everlasting covenant."

Look back and see the burden Jesus bore, lay your hand of faith on His holy head and confess your sins, and the curse will be removed and you can say, believing, I rejoice to see the curse removed. "We bless the Lamb with cheerful voice and sing his bleeding love."

www.ingramcontent.com/pod-product-compliance
Lightning Source LLC
La Vergne TN
LVHW091226180726
843490LV00006B/1949